MOVING TO GREATER FORT MYERS

THE UN-TOURIST GUIDE®

LAURA PIERCE HESS

Moving to Greater Fort Myers
The Un-Tourist Guide®

Cover design and interior layout by www.PearCreative.ca

Cover Image Courtesy of Prima Luce, the downtown Fort Myers high rise developers: Visit them online: www.primalucelife.com

Printed in the U.S.A
Print ISBN: 978-0-9996478-8-2
Ebook ISBN: 978-0-9996478-9-9

CONTENTS

Chapter 4

What To Explore Outdoors?

Chapter 5

The Art of Shopping, Dining, and Entertainment

FOREWORD

BY KELLIE BURNS, NBC-2 NEWS EVENING ANCHOR

I moved to Fort Myers in August of 1993 at the age of 28. I packed up my sports car with just clothing and drove 24 hours to Florida from Upstate New York. I had taken a job, sight unseen, at Waterman Broadcasting, the NBC station and honestly, the only thing I knew about the area was that it was on the West Coast of Florida, somewhere between Naples and Tampa.

Back then this was a small tourist town, made up of mostly retirees. Six months of the year, The City of Palms was a virtual ghost town. About half the residents were seasonal, and many businesses shut down for six months of the year. Safe to say, the average age was well beyond my years, but as I drove over the Caloosahatchee into downtown I was smitten. I loved this city nestled into the river, the art deco buildings, the brick streets, eclectic restaurants, and the smell of salt water.

Fast forward nearly 25 years, and this tiny tourist town has grown to more than half a million people. In television terms, we have jumped from market 96 to market 56, based on our population doubling in just a quarter century. The median age is now just 45 years old.

The area has grown in large part because it's now drawing families and professionals. Chico's and Arthrex are head-quartered here. Golisano Children's Hospital offers top notch health care in an incredible new facility. Florida Gulf Coast University and Florida Southwestern State bring in world class educators and students from across the globe. Our airport is one of the busiest in the southeast. Wow, how far we have come. We became famous for our Dunk City basketball team making it to the Sweet 16. Baseball is our hometown sport, with the Red Sox and Twins training here in the Spring.

All this playing out in front of the most spectacular backdrop. The beauty of our beaches, islands, and waterways are unparalleled. A drive over the Sanibel causeway at sunset, with a Pelican racing alongside your car on the c span bridge, is a spiritual experience. Shelling at sunrise on the white sandy beaches of Sanibel, sunset on Captiva with a cocktail from the Mucky Duck, lunch at the Collier Inn on Useppa Island, camping on Cayo Costa—so much beauty right in my backyard.

Take a jog down McGregor Boulevard, under the Royal Palm lined corridor, hike Koreshan State Park where the founders established their version of Utopia, bike Ding Darling National Wildlife refuge or walk the boardwalk at the Six Mile Cypress Slough. Parades, festivals, theaters, art galleries, parks, and historical sites round out the list of things to do.

Honestly, when I moved here at the age of 28, I thought it would be a stopover to a big city and a larger television market, but at the end of my first contract, I knew I did not want to live anywhere else. I loved the smell of the warm salt air, even the humidity felt good. No this was home. My children rarely wear shoes, do not own winter coats, and learned to swim before they could walk.

..and that is just the way we like it.

INTRODUCTION

WHY EVERYONE LOVES GREATER FORT MYERS, FLORIDA

"There is only one Fort Myers in the United States,
and there are 90 million people who are going to find out about it"

THOMAS A. EDISON 1914, *FORT MYERS PRESS*

Fort Myers Pier at Sunset

Congratulations on finding paradise! The inspirational natural beauty of our city was not lost on the brilliant mind of Thomas Edison. In his day Fort Myers lacked most, if not all, of the modern conveniences we enjoy today. But his presence and vision in the small town of Fort Myers fueled an ongoing growth and development that still continues. Today, Fort Myers is one of many wonderful communities in Lee County that offer wonderful weather and a marvelous lifestyle.

It's easy to see the reason that so many people visit once, vacation several times, and then finally make a home in the Fort Myers area. For centuries explorers, innovators, vacationers, and families have been drawn to the natural beauty and charm of this area. From Ponce de Leon rumored findings of the Fountain of Youth to Thomas Edison's lush experimental gardens and laboratory, it is undeniable we live in a special place.

Top 10 Reasons to Move to Greater Fort Myers

1. Winterless Weather

Florida isn't called the Sunshine state for nothing. With an average of 271 days of sunshine a year, there is no need for heavy-duty snowsuits, mittens or boots here. Our summers are hot and humid, but brief daily afternoon showers bring cooler evenings. Everywhere you go has air-conditioning—businesses, homes, and cars—so you don't need to worry about melting! Fall brings cooler temperatures, enough to warrant wearing a sweater, perhaps a light jacket along with a pair of fashionable boots, while you sit around the fire with friends or walking on the beach.

2. Waterfront Wonderland

Lee County boasts over 600 miles of shorelines, with some of the most beautiful beaches in the world. Our beaches are repeatedly recognized in global publications as the best in the world. Great beaches bring great shelling. In 2012 at the 75th annual Sanibel Shell Show & Fair residents and visitors broke the Guinness World Record for the largest shell scavenger hunt by doing the "Sanibel Stoop". Cape Coral's 400 miles of canals constitute more canals than anywhere in the world. The waterfront homes in Cape Coral are highly desired by recreational boaters, fisherman, and those that enjoy the natural beauty of living on the water.

3. Cozy Communities

Lee County encompasses a large area of 1212 square miles with several large and small cities, towns, villages, and neighborhoods within the county lines. Each one has its own distinct personality and style, but even our largest cities have a great small town feel to them. Cape Coral is the largest city in Lee County and is a diverse melting pot of residents from around the globe. Pine Island, North Fort Myers, Alva, and Buckingham offer an old Florida county feel. In the southeast, you will find Gateway, Lehigh Acres, Estero, Bonita Springs that are close to many of our shopping and sports centers. The diversity within our county is one of the reasons I wrote this book.

4. Affordable Cost of Living

The cost of living and doing business in Lee County is extremely attractive for individuals, families, companies relocating, and entrepreneurs. Well-priced homes, low property taxes, reasonable utility costs, and no state income tax make living here quite affordable.

5. Pleasant Polite People

Maybe it is the steady stream of Midwesterners who have moved down to Lee County over the years or maybe it is the gentle pace of living that has populated Lee County with some of the kindest and happiest people I know. In 2013 Coastal living voted Sanibel as one of the top 3 "happiest seaside town". It's no wonder anytime I need a dose of happiness, I head out to Sanibel for a sunset and I feel recharged!

6. Wild About Wildlife

The Audubon Society of Southwest Florida, Turtle Time Monitoring Organization, Corkscrew Wildlife Sanctuary, Ding Darling Wildlife Refuge, and Conservancy of Southwest Florida are just a few of the dedicated groups that care for and protect the wildlife of Florida. Getting involved with these groups is tremendously rewarding and offers you an inside look into the beautiful animals, birds, and fish that live alongside us in Southwest Florida.

7. Philanthropic Paradise

Generosity is golden in the sunshine state. Southwest Florida attracts a generous group of givers that help improve our community. The

Southwest Florida Community Foundation helps charitable dollars go to the causes that have the most need. Whether your passion is people, animals, education, environment, arts or economic development there are ways you can be a "change maker". Lee County is a terrific place to get involved and to feel like YOU can make a difference.

8. Highest Healthcare Standards

Lee County has a wide array of quality healthcare resources from acute care hospitals to expert children's care, cardiology, and orthopedics. Lee Health is the 6th largest system in the United States. HealthGrades. com also named Lee Memorial Hospital and HealthPark Medical Center among America's 50 Best Hospitals, which is among the top 1% of hospitals nationwide[1]. All the staff, doctors, and nurses are exceptionally caring and helpful at both HealthPark Medical Center and Gulf Coast Hospital.

9. Educational Excellence

You'll find what you need from pre-K to graduate school in Lee County. The Lee County School District is the 36th largest district in the US and is committed to quality, unity, and diversity throughout the county. The educational community has worked tirelessly to bring technology, STEM, arts, college prep, and trade courses to all schools. In addition, several post high school education options can put you and your children on the path to a great career.

10. Great Place to Retire and Great Place to Raise a Family

Just a quick look around will show you that Lee County is a magnet for retirees. Lee County communities are commonly noted as a best place to live in several different publications. Cape Coral was listed as #8 of the 25 Best Places to Retire in 2018 by Forbes[2] and Marketwatch.com listed Fort Myers as one of the top 10 Best US Cities to Retire.[3] Raising a family here has also been mentioned in a book "50 Fabulous Places to Raise Your Family" by Kathleen Shaputis and DestinationSeeker.com listed Fort Myers as one of the top 15 Places to Live in Florida, specifically mentioning that it was a great place to raise a family.

CHAPTER 1

HISTORY OF FORT MYERS

Original Inhabitants

Native Americans have inhabited the state of Florida for thousands of years. Approximately 7000 years ago people began living in villages around the wetlands and coastal areas. People concentrated in areas that could provide easier access to food sources, and the abundance of seafood resources in the waters of Southwest Florida become an attractive settlement area.

One of the indigenous cultures in Southwest Florida that we know the most about were the Calusa, or "fierce people" in their language. The Calusa society ranged from the coastal areas of Estero Bay northward to Charlotte Harbor. This culture relied heavily on the fish from the estuaries as well as the shellfish such as oysters. The large shell middens which accumulated over generations can still be seen at places such as Mound Key State Park in Estero Bay. Many experts believe Mound Key to be the capital of the Calusa, and evidence of their culture has been dated to approximately 1150 B.C. Their extensive history still remains and can be explored at this underappreciated State Park, which can only be accessed by boat.

European Contact

The first recorded contact between Europeans and the Calusa was in 1513, when Juan Ponce de Leon landed on the west coast of Florida. They were eventually driven off land, and on his last trip to Florida in

1521 the expedition landed somewhere around the Caloosahatchee River and they were again attacked. Because of this altercation Ponce de Leon was wounded by an arrow and died shortly after in Cuba.

There was sporadic contact between the Spanish and Calusa over the next century and much of what we know of their society comes from a memory written by Hernando de Escalante Fontaneda who was a Spanish shipwreck survivor who lived among the Calusa for 17 years. Hernando was rescued around 1566 and his account, written in 1575, is one of the only contemporary documents of Ponce de Leon's famous search for the Fountain of Youth.

By the time Spain lost control of Florida in 1763, disease and conflict had caused the decline of the Calusa and other indigenous populations in Florida and the remaining Calusa tribes effectively ceased to exist.

HISTORY'S MYSTERY - Sanibel and Captiva Islands are rumored to be named after Queen Isabella of Spain "Santa Isybella" and from Pirate Jose Gaspar's buried stolen treasure on Sanibel and kept female prisoners "Captive" on the "Isle de los Captivas" or Captiva Island.

First American Settlers (1800's-1900's)

In 1821, Florida became a part of US territory. Families headed south to settle in the newly acquired land, but this land was occupied by the native Seminoles which led to tension that inevitably started the Seminole Indian Wars. Major General David E. Twiggs sent one of his majors to select a site along the Caloosahatchee. The fort would be called "Fort Myers". The reason behind the name is a heartfelt one. General Twiggs daughter Marion was in love and engaged to be married to Col. Abraham C. Myers, a Chief Quartermaster of the Department of Florida.

Between 1863-1865 Fort Myers was the location for the southernmost land battle of the American Civil War. It was a Union occupied base, rare for being so far south. Close to 300 soldiers were assigned to protect cattle. This precious commodity of cattle fed the troops, so having control of the cattle meant controlling the battles. The confederate soldiers did not stick around long with no food available to them. The battle of Fort Myers was fought and won on

February 20th, 1865. You can find a recently refurbished historical marker at the downtown Fort Myers/Lee County Library location (2450 First St., Fort Myers). The old fort was abandoned after the end of the Civil War.

Pioneer and Spanish Trading Ship Captain Manual A. Gonzalez along with his 5-year-old son, Manual S. Gonzalez, and brother-in-law John Weatherford were the first permanent settlers in Fort Myers on February 21st, 1866. Weatherford returned to Key West to bring back the Captain's wife Evelina, daughter Mary Gonzalez along with their adopted daughter Christina Stirrup Vivas and new husband Joseph.

Manny Gonzalez Home Built in 1902

The Gonzalez family had been mail and supply runners to the fort during the Seminole War. Manual and his family rebuilt what was left of the old fort and eventually moved to an area he named "Manuel's Branch," which is landmarked today with a quaint old bridge, beautifully shaded park, and small creek that runs from the Caloosahatchee River behind Manuel Drive to the rear of Fort Myers High School. In 1902 his son Manny built a home for his family at the corner of Second Street and Broadway, and 1912 he built a home next door for his now widowed mother Evelina. These two houses are now connected as one building and survive today as home to one of Fort Myers finest and historic restaurants, "The Veranda".

The Veranda Restaurant Today

Around 1867 the next settlers started moving to Fort Myers. William S. Clay from Tennessee was one of them. The Clay family first squatted on the riverfront between Monroe and Hendry Street before deciding to make moonshine. They set up a sugar cane whiskey still along a creek southwest of downtown. This creek became known as Whiskey Creek. It is located in the subdivision of the same name where all the streets have alcohol-related names.

Slowly more families moved to the old Fort, picking up the pieces of the destroyed and abandoned buildings, and planting new gardens and crops. Farming, cattle, and logging had been the main industry in Fort Myers in the early days of incorporation. It encouraged many of the early settlers to set up homesteads along the Caloosahatchee and inland to better work the land and ship their goods. Wealthy cattle herder and landholder, Jacob Summerlin, had over 15,000 head of cattle and owned thousands of acres in the region, including the Punta Rassa Wharf. Summerlin Road follows the "Cracker Trail" on which these herders brought their cattle from Fort Pierce to the Wharf at Punta Rassa.

With the cattle came the cash that powered prosperity. Cattlemen and their families came to Fort Myers to buy supplies from merchants, blacksmiths, cobblers, and to get help from a druggist or doctor when needed. The free land offered by the Homestead Act of 1862 brought northerners south to claim land.

National headlines were made in 1885 when famous inventor Thomas Alva Edison made his way from St Augustine down to Southwest Florida. He was so enamored with Fort Myers that he eventually bought 13 acres on the Caloosahatchee that would become his winter residence. "Seminole Lodge," Edison's winter home, was completed in 1886 and electric lights illuminated for the first time on March 27th 1887.

Thomas Edison Winter Residence "Seminole Lodge"
Courtesy of the Edison Ford Winter Estates

Over the years, the Edison's would invite a variety of friends and associates to share the beautiful warm weather of Southwest Florida. Well known friends such as the Henry Ford and Harvey Firestone's would make their way to Fort Myers to visit and even set up winter residences alongside Edison's Seminole Lodge.

Henry Ford Winter Residence "The Mangoes".
Courtesy of the Edison Ford Winter Estates

Other wealthy families followed suit. In 1901 Nelson & Adeline Burroughs built a Georgian Revival Mansion on the Caloosahatchee River and First Street. Eventually, the city and Uncommon Friends Foundation would take ownership of this magnificent home which is now a historical landmark, museum, and site for many weddings and events including the spectacular Holiday House put on by the Fort Myers Women's Community Club.

Historical Burroughs Residence
decorated for its Annual Holiday House

Notable visitors that have been drawn to Southwest Florida include five US Presidents: George H.W. Bush, George W. Bush, Jimmy Carter, Herbert Hoover, and Theodore Roosevelt have all vacationed around the Gulf Waters of Southwest Florida (abbreviated ahead as SWFL).

The beauty of our area has been an inspiration for many authors and artists like Pulitzer Prize winners Edna St Vincent Millay (poet), along with Anne Marrow Lindbergh (author of Gift from the Sea) and J.N. "Ding" Darling (conversationalist and renowned editorial cartoonist).

Fascinating Fort Myers Facts

- In a small log cabin located near the riverbank in January 1872 Methodist traveling clergy members came to town to hold the first church service for the 4 families that lived here.

- In that same small log cabin in the winter of 1873, the first paid teacher would hold school for 10 Fort Myers children.

- Stafford Cleveland moved to Fort Myers and launched the *Fort Myers Press* 1884.

- City of Fort Myers was incorporated on August 12th, 1885. At the time, it had a population of only 349 residents but was still the second largest town on the Gulf Coast of Florida south of Cedar Key.

- 1887 a bill was passed to separate from Monroe County and become Lee County, which was named after General Robert E. Lee.

- Also in 1887 Lee County become a dry county, resulting in the closing of 2 saloons, but it was a big boost for business for good ole Bill Clay who was able to peddle his moonshine to residents in need.

- Tamiami Trail Bridge was built in 1924 and ushered the first real estate boom. But, the great depression created the first bust.

PAVING THE WAY FOR FORT MYERS FUTURE - One of the first main streets in Fort Myers is McGregor Boulevard. It was the main road that was traveled from the downtown business district to the trading docks of the Punta Rassa wharf. It was named after the McGregor family. Ambrose and Tootie McGregor along with their son Bradford moved from Kings County, New York, and purchased the west half of Edison's Seminole Lodge in 1892. Tootie's irritation with the cattle worn road conditions in Fort Myers spurred her to fund a paving project. McGregor Boulevard is the outcome of her generosity and pride, as she required naming rights when she funded the project. The fountain that sits in front of the Edison Restaurant at the Fort Myers County Club was also donated by the McGregor family and has a quote written by Tootie that reads, *"I only hope the little I have done may be an incentive to others to do more."*

City of Palms McGregor Boulevard

Southwest Florida historic landmarks are not always obvious to the untrained eye, so here is a list of some of my favorite cultural and historical noteworthy places to visit:

- Edison Winter Home "Seminole Lodge" built in 1886

- Ford's Winter Home "Mangos"

- The Veranda Restaurant which is made up of 2 turn of the century homes that were built in the 1860s by early settlers, the Gonzales Family.

- Koreshan Unity Settlement in Estero built in 1894

- Gasparilla Inn & Club Boca Grande built in 1913

- Burroughs Home & Garden Fort Myers built in 1901

- Mound Key (accessible by small water craft, boat, kayak) in Estero Bay

- 'Tween Waters Inn on Captiva built in 1931

- Sidney & Berne Davis Arts Center built in 1933 in Downtown Fort Myers is a Neoclassical Revival architectural masterpiece with large vertical columns made of Florida Limestone. This former government building was left in disrepair until an extensive renovation was completed in 2014.

Taking a "True Tours" of Downtown Fort Myers Historical District is a wonderful way travel back in time to see how Fort Myers grew to the city it is today.

- Sanibel Light House built in 1884

- Casa Ybel Resort & Thistle Lodge built in the mid 1880's

Casa Ybel Resort Now

Growth of Paradise (1900's-Present)

Building expansion in Fort Myers started as early as 1898 and on through the 1920's when Florida became a destination for those seeking to escape the cold northern winter weather for some sunshine. Land investors followed suit and had a huge impact on making Southwest Florida what it is today. In 1915 the battle between "The Tamiami Trail vs. the Cross State Highway" began and powerful businessman Barron Collier, who lived in Fort Myers during that time, fought with all of his political and business advertising influence along with a private investment of 1 million dollars to secure that the new east-west corridor that connected Tampa to Miami would go through Southwest Florida. If it wasn't for Barron Collier's efforts the East-West Corridor connecting Tampa and Miami would have run through Arcadia, leaving the gulf coast scarcely populated.

Tamiami Trailblazers
Photo: State Archives of Florida

During World War II Fort Myers had 2 airbases. Page Field & Buckingham airbases created a mini population boom for our area once the war ended. The returning servicemen sprawled out across the county creating the start of many of our towns and cities including Cape Coral, North Fort Myers, Lehigh Acres, Fort Myers Beach, Bonita Springs, Sanibel, Captiva, and Pine Island.

The post war boom continued its upward population trajectory. Beautiful weather and bountiful resources created the tourism industry and inexpensive land along with low taxes made it a magnet for anyone with ambitions and vision to create the much-needed infrastructure to support visitors and settlers. This cycle of increased visitors who turned into year-round residents, which, then attracted businesses to support the increased population is a business model that continues to work to this day.

In 1983 Southwest Florida Regional Airport was opened off Daniels Parkway just east of Interstate 75, making tourism not just easier for Americans but also international guests. Just one year after opening it started servicing international flights. RSW became Southwest Florida International Airport in 1993 and made Southwest Florida an international destination.

CHAPTER 2

GETTING TO KNOW GREATER FORT MYERS AND LEE ISLAND COAST.

Nicknames, Towns, and Cities of Lee County

Lee County includes several cities and towns. When choosing your home, consider:

- Where will you be spending a majority of your time (work, school, hobbies)?

- Find out what your commute time will be in both summer and winter months.

Minimizing travel times will maximize the time you get to enjoy Southwest Florida from places other than your car!

Lee County and the surrounding area is often referred to as Gulf Coast, Lee Island Coast, Southwest Florida, and even Royal Palm Coast. It is made up of several governing municipalities and hundreds of community associations that set rules for its given area. Here are some of the larger governing bodies: The City of Fort Myers, City of Bonita Springs, City of Cape Coral, City of Sanibel, Town of Fort Myers Beach, and the Village of Estero.

It is entirely possible to move to Fort Myers but not actually live "in" the city of Fort Myers. Much of Lee County is considered unincorporated, but there are many popular areas to get to know.

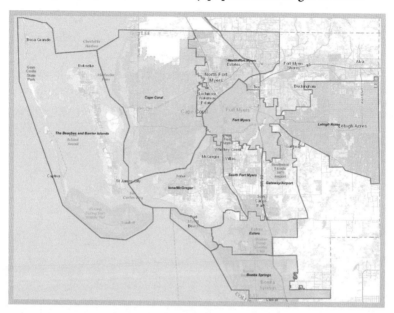

Getting Around by Car (Roadways)

Traveling by car is the best way to get around our area. Although public transportation is an option, its limitations will take you a long time to get to your intended destination.

Let's explore the four areas of Lee County, show you how to navigate our roadways, and introduce you to the main communities. The major roadways in Lee County are fairly simple. **Interstate 75** and **US Highway 41** are the 2 main thoroughfares running north-south parallel with the coastline.

- **Interstate 75** will take you from the Charlotte county line to Collier County line quickly. So, when you need to go from one side of the county to the other and you are near the interstate, it is an easy way to cut through the county.

- **US Highway 41** is the main business thoroughfare in Fort Myers which make it a congested thoroughfare to drive on. It is also called Tamiami Trail as the road originally connected Tampa to Miami.

Vacationers and commercial vehicles increase traffic significantly during the winter months. So just remember to get on the road a bit early and be patient. If you are not accustomed to commuting long distances to work, it would be beneficial to choose your home location based on the area you will be working or spending most your time.

Local Toll Road Tip: Lee County only has 3 tolls and they are located on the westbound lanes of the Sanibel Causeway Bridge, Cape Coral Bridge, and Veterans Memorial Bridge (also referred to as the Midpoint Bridge). Save time and possibly money when you are a frequent traveler by purchasing a LeeWay www.leegov.com/dot/tolls or SunPass transponder www.sunpass.com. Each program has reciprocal agreements with other toll facilities. Check out the websites to see which one would work best for you and your future travels.

City of Fort Myers

The City of Fort Myers is our county seat and houses many of our government office buildings. Downtown, our Fort Myers River District has grown to include many shops, restaurants, high-rise and low-rise residential condos along with several historic single-family homes. If you are heading downtown for an event visit www.myriverdistrict.com for a map, general parking information, special events parking and trolley routes.

State Road 867 (McGregor Boulevard), US 41 (Cleveland Avenue), First Street, State Road 80 (Palm Beach Boulevard) State Road 82 (Martin Luther King Blvd) radiate out from the center of Downtown Fort Myers and branch out into the rest of the county.

Northern Lee County Roadways:

- **Burnt Store Road** runs parallel to the Gulf in the North part of the county from Pine Island Road in Cape Coral all the way up to Burnt Store Marina at the Charlotte County line. Burnt Store Road turns into Veterans Memorial Parkway at south of Pine Island Road. Veterans will take a turn to the east and bring you all the way to Fort Myers via the Veterans Memorial Bridge (toll required west bound lanes only).

- **State Road 78** is also known as Pine Island Road. It will take you from Pine Island, through Cape Coral, North Fort Myers, and turn into Bayshore Road after the old 41 intersection and all the way out to US 31.

- **US Highway 31** will take you out to Babcock Ranch and the new all solar city that is being built. It will also take you to historic Arcadia.

East Lee County Roadways:

- **State Roads 80** (Palm Beach Boulevard) will take you from downtown to Labelle and Hendry County

- **State Road 82** (Martin Luther King Boulevard) will take you from downtown through Lehigh Acres to Immokalee.

- **State Road 884** is called **Colonial Boulevard** on the west side of SR 82 and then turns into Lee Road on the east side of SR 82.

- **State road 873** (Joel Boulevard) travels from the north at Palm Beach Boulevard south into Lehigh Acres.

- **Buckingham Road** connects SR 80 to SR 82.

- **Gateway Boulevard** connects SR 82 with **Daniels Parkway** at the backside of the Southwest Florida International Airport.

- **Daniels Parkway** connects US 41 all the way to Gateway Boulevard.

- **Alico Road** connects US 41 with Corkscrew Road

- **Treeline Avenue/Ben Hill Griffin Parkway** is a great north/south road that lies just a couple blocks east of I-75, running parallel between Colonial to Corkscrew.

Western Lee County Roadways:

A majority of Western Lee County is made up of our largest city, Cape Coral. This city's roads and canals have been painstakingly planned out. Here's a primer to understanding the basics.

- **Del Prado Boulevard, Santa Barbara Boulevard, Skyline Boulevard, Chiquita Boulevard**, all bisect through Cape Coral in a North-South direction.

- **Cape Coral Parkway, Veterans Parkway, Viscaya Parkway, Trafalgar Parkway** all run East to West in Cape Coral.

- East/West roads are called Parkways, Streets, Terraces, Lanes

- North/South roads are Boulevards, Courts, Places and Avenues.

Make sure to have a map and GPS handy while navigating the Cape in the beginning; it can be a sanity saver. Waterways in the Cape can be just as confusing as roadways, so if you are buying a waterfront home in the Cape it is important to you make sure you consult with a waterfront Realtor® specialist who can give you a clear understanding of the canal access points to open water, if the canal is land locked, has weirs, bridges or locks. All these factors can affect your boating enjoyment. The City of Cape Corals website has great maps: http://capecoral.net/i_want_to1/find/maps/index.php#.WFgSnHeZNsY.

Southern Lee County Roadways:

- **McGregor Boulevard (State Road 867)** starts in downtown Fort Myers near the Edison Ford Estates and follows the river all the way to the intersection of Gladiolus and San Carlos Boulevard. At this intersection, you must make a right turn to stay on McGregor Boulevard and make your way to the Sanibel Causeway (Punta Rassa).

- If you continue south on **San Carlos Boulevard (SR 865)**, you will find yourself on Fort Myers Beach (Estero Island).

- **Summerlin Road (SR 869)** runs parallel to US 41 from Colonial Boulevard to the McGregor Boulevard and then to Sanibel Causeway.

- **Winkler Road** runs from McGregor Boulevard through South Fort Myers passed Summerlin Road to a cul-de-sac road that ends at the Estero Bay Preserve.

- **Colonial Boulevard** (Veterans Parkway Bridge Connection) east/west road

- **College Parkway** (Cape Coral Bridge Connection) east/west road

- **Cypress Lake Drive** starts at McGregor runs west to US 41 where it turns into **Daniels Parkway.**

- **Gladiolus Drive** is the gateway to the beaches from US 41. It can be someone congested near the US 41 Intersection.

- **Three Oaks Parkway** connects Alico Road to Coconut Road (Coconut Point Mall) and Imperial Parkway on to Bonita Beach Road.

- **Corkscrew Road** can take you from US 41 all the way through Estero to SR 82 near Immokalee.

- **Bonita Beach Road** goes from the Gulfcoast on the West to I 75 in the east.

Summing Up

There are hundreds of communities and subdivisions small and large all over Lee County. It takes about an hour to go from one side of the county to the other, so find out before your move how long commute times will be during tourist season. That will give you more time to enjoy all the wonderful things Lee Island Coast has to offer.

Getting Out of Town (Air Travel)

RSW Runways and Terminal

The Gulf Coast of Florida has a never-ending list of places to explore and things to do but if you are looking for a change of scenery, Southwest Florida International (RSW) makes leaving town a breeze. It is centrally located in Lee County and can be easily accessed by exit 128 on I-75 or by Treeline Avenue. Recently, RSW was named one of the top 50 US airports for passenger traffic. Here are more details from 2017:

- 48 non-stop domestic destinations

- 6 international destinations

International destinations include Montreal, Ottawa, Toronto, Dusseldorf, Cancun, and San Juan. Visit www.flylcpa.com for the most up to date travel information.

The Lee County Port Authority (LCPA) operates Southwest Florida International Airport and Page Field Airport (KFMY). Page Field Airport is located off of US 41 near the intersection of Colonial. It ranks in the top 20% of Base Operations, which offer convenient concierge service for travelers, pilots, and crew of smaller private aircrafts. There is a second Base Operations in Lee County called PrivateSky that operates out of the RSW airstrip and can handle larger airplanes and jets.

Southwest Florida International Airport (RSW)
11000 Terminal Access Road
Fort Myers, FL 33913
Phone: 239-590-4800
www.flylcpa.com

Page Field Airport (KFMY) Base Operations
5200 Captain Channing Page Drive
Fort Myers, FL 33907
Phone: 239-590-6600
www.baseoperationsfmy.com

PrivateSky Aviation (RSW) Base Operations
One PrivateSky Way
Fort Myers, Florida 33913
Phone: 239-225-6100
www.privatesky.net

CHAPTER 3

HOW'S THE WEATHER?

Lee County Seasons

People flock here for our weather. It may be because they are so sick of shoveling snow that they can't do it one more day or because they dream of having dozens more days of sunlight and blue skies than grey overcast ones.

There are two main seasons in Fort Myers: summer and winter. You will enjoy not having to shovel snow off your car for either season! Our area is considered the subtropics, so you can expect hot and muggy weather and daily rains during the summer and spring months.

Spring and Summer Season

Summers are hot and humid for sure. Fort Myers rarely breaks national heat index records, which the dryer desert cities are prone to do. We do tend to make lists for the amount of days we have over 90 degrees. If you are not used to a humid heat it will take a little getting used to. Almost every business, home, and car has air conditioning. So during the summer months you might find yourself like me wearing a lightweight sweater over a tank top because I will get chilly from the air conditioning!

Every place has its weather warnings, and here are a few for the spring and summer months:

- Hyperthermia: Make sure to stay hydrated if you are exercising, playing sports, or doing outside activities. The heat can escalate your body temperature to deadly levels.

- Don't leave pets or children in the car unattended any time of year here. Children and pets are less able to regulate body temperature to keep cool, so even a short period in the car on what appears to be a mild weather day can have catastrophic outcome.

- Florida is the lightning capital of the US, so *"When the Thunder Roars, Go Indoors"*, as lightning can strike far before the storm arrives. Get out of the water, off the fields, put away electric devices, and make sure to go inside as soon as you hear the thunder of an approaching storm.

It will feel like summer from about May through Mid-October in Florida. High temps hit from the mid to high 90s. Rainfall can be heavy at times. The total annual precipitation is 55 inches. Most of it falls during the spring and summer months.

Average Monthly High & Low Temperature for Fort Myers Area

Month	Jan	Feb	Mar	Apr	May	Jun
Average High (F)	73.5	74.4	77.1	79.2	82.4	84.5
Average Low (F)	50	52.2	57.5	64.6	71.8	76.3
Month	Jul	Aug	Sep	Oct	Nov	Dec
Average High (F)	85	85.3	84.2	81.9	77.7	74.7
Average Low (F)	78	78.5	76.5	67.7	57.3	51.3

Temperature for Fort Myers Area
Courtesy of NOWData NOAA Online Weather Data

Winter and Fall Season

Our fall and winter weather is mild compared the rest of the US. The coldest month on average is January, but the record low was 24 degrees in December of 1894 according to Intellicast.com. Fort Myers has seen frosts and even a rare light snowfall that melts on touching the ground.

Typical temperatures during the fall and winter months will range from the 70s-80s during the day to the 50s and 60s at night. Every day is a great day to be outside enjoying the beach or boating out on the water. The cool breezy nights are delightful opportunities for enjoying the stars with a glass of your favorite wine and friends.

Brief cold fronts are actually a luxury for most residents, reminding us of the cold that we left behind. It gives us the opportunity to turn on our heaters and burn the dust off the coils. (Note: You may smell a faint burning smell when you first turn your heater on, this is normal) It also allows us to enjoy some sweater weather! Winter wear consists of a sweater or a light coat, paired with pants or jeans, and of course some fashionable loafers or boots to complete the look. The key to our cold weather is layers—because the heat index during the day could make the 80s degree average feel like 90s. And wind chills can make the 50s feel like the 40s. Occasionally, I will use a light fashion scarf and gloves to keep warm, but that typically occurs when I am doing something outdoors like enjoying a nice bonfire or perhaps participating in an outdoor concert, sporting event or activity.

There is nothing too extreme about our seasons, but you don't have to take my word for it. Usnews.com named Florida one of the top 10 retirement spots in the US with Year-Round Nice Weather. That's one of many statistics that reference our beautiful Southwest Florida climate.

The Reality of Hurricanes

Every city has its nature/weather challenges, and Fort Myers is no exception. Although very rare, hurricanes and tropical storms are a part of the natural weather patterns in Southwest Florida. So, you must be aware and prepare for these events.

So, when is the right time to get ready? Right now! As soon as you decide to move is when you should start to make your plan—especially if your move will hit hurricane season from June 1 to November 30.

First step – Get educated, because knowledge is the key to safety. Pretty much every news station, newspaper, city, and township will create a printed and online hurricane guide for residents and visitors. These are very helpful resources for you to keep in your home. I like to have one from a major news station, one from the county, and also one from the National Hurricane Center (which is a part of the Nation Oceanic and Atmospheric Administration www.nhc.noaa.gov). Between these three sources, you will have up to date information about evacuation routes, shelter locations, and start to learn the new weather lingo like "eye wall" or "millibars". Last but not least, visit the Florida Office of Insurance Regulation website (www.floir.com/sections/pandc/floodinsurance/floodinsurance.aspx) to understand how Flood Insurance works and how to get it.

Second Step: Have a personal hurricane plan. Once you have compiled and reviewed your hurricane guides, it is time to complete the hurricane homework that most of those guides include. Purchase your hurricane supplies (batteries, water, canned food, etc), determine the materials you may want to have for your home, like hurricane shutters, plywood or generators. Talk to your neighbors, your employer, and your children's schools to find out how they handle their plans. This can help you implement your plan as well. It's also important to identify evacuation routes and shelters.

Third Step: Stay informed and be ready to act. Meteorologists on every channel will be forecasting where the tropical storms or hurricanes will be heading each season. Typically, hurricanes are formed somewhere in-between the warm waters of the tip of Africa and follow the Gulf Stream through to the Caribbean and toward North America. The Atlantic Hurricane season runs from June 1st through November 30th when the waters are at their warmest. Meteorologists create "spaghetti maps" to forecast which areas might be affected, but like any weather event, it is best to stay tuned to watch for the most current forecast until the weather threat has passed.

Fourth Step: Relax. You Are Now Prepared. Now it is time to hit the beach, golf courses, and parks to enjoy the reason why you moved here! Our weather is absolutely glorious a majority of the time, so don't let hurricane season scare you away from the beauty of our waterfront wonderland.

CHAPTER 4

WHAT TO EXPLORE OUTDOORS?

"With over 590 miles of coastline, over 100 islands, 50 miles of white sand beaches, unique and diverse ecosystems, and 25 nature preserves and parks, there are many choices about what to see and do."
Quote from the Lee County Visitor & Convention Bureau.

At The Beaches

A Lovely Fort Myers Beach

Our beautiful beaches are one of Lee County's best assets. People across the globe come here to enjoy our award-winning beaches. Now that you are on your way to becoming a resident, it's time to get the inside tips on how to get the most out of our beaches!

Best Local Beaches

- **Bowman Beach Park** (Sanibel Island) offers a lot of parking, amenities, and a large beach area to get a quiet spot and look for the best shells. You'll learn why the Sanibel Stoop is popular position on the beach.

- **Barefoot Beach** (Bonita Springs) also has a lot of parking and amenities with pristine sprawling powder white beaches.

- **Cape Coral Yacht Club** (Cape Coral) is equipped with a restaurant and bar right on the water, along with a small beach and playground for the kids. It is the best of both worlds for adults and kids!

- **Bunche Beach** (Fort Myers) has the best beach for exploring tidal pools. The constant tidal flow creates an ever-changing scene for nature lovers to walk the tidal flats. The parking area is on the street entrance and there are no beach bathrooms which make it an ideal place for a short beach stop.

- **Lovers Key** is one of the most visited State Parks in the State of Florida. They host 300 talks and tours each year. Nature lovers will love this little island. It offers hiking, paddling, nature walks and beautiful beaches.

- **Bowditch Beach Park** (Fort Myers Beach) has abundant parking and amenities in a park like setting. It is located on the north tip of Estero Island.

Fort Myers Beach also has over 25 Beach Access Points nestled in between quiet residential streets all along Estero Boulevard. They are easily recognizable by the signs and can give you quick access to non-crowded beach areas. If you live in South Lee County consider driving in on the Bonita Beach Road to avoid the San Carlos Boulevard traffic.

There is no way to avoid beach traffic completely. The roads to the beaches will swell with cars during season, so you need to start your day early or plan to go later in the afternoon to avoid the worst of the traffic. It's also a good idea to pack a picnic lunch or dinner or consider eating during non-peak times to avoid long waits at the island and beach restaurants

Dog Friendly Beaches

On the southern tip of Lovers Key, you will find a beach that is literally "for the dogs". Dog Beach allows for your 4-legged family members to roam FREE and unleashed! This beach makes Fort Myers one of the most dog loving cities in Florida. Leashed dogs are allowed on most other Lee County Public Beaches, just remember to clean up after your pooch - so we can continue to be a dog friendly area.

TIME SAVER IDEA:
Save yourself the time and money with a "Lee County Beach & Parks Annual Parking Sticker" for $60. You will have access to parking at 18 different park locations throughout Lee County. No need to hassle with parking ticket stubs and remembering when your parking stub expires. www.leegov.com/parks/parking

At The Parks

Koreshan State Park: A Wonderful Place to Wander

The county is dedicated to creating parks that enhance not only visitors experience here, but the residents too. Our city parks (www. leegov.com/parks) host community events, farmers markets, and art fairs, while our Conservation 20/20 Lands

(www.leegov.com/conservation2020) created 45 nature preserves that protect the ecosystem and create a peaceful place for all of us to view wildlife sightings, enjoy hiking trails, biking, equestrian rides, and picnicking. Here's a short list of favorites that you should visit:

Best Local Parks and Preserves

- **Manatee Park** is where you will find many manatees during the winter months. Take Exit 141 on I-75 east to park entrance.

- **Caloosahatchee Regional Park** offers equestrian trails, mountain bike trails, and primitive camping and kayak launch on the Caloosahatchee River in Alva. This land is exquisite and must be experienced!

- **Six Mile Cypress Slough Preserve and Interpretive Center** is centrally located on Six Mile Cypress between Daniels and Colonial. You will learn what exactly a "slough" is and, more importantly, how to pronounce it like a local. It's pronounced "Slew", like stew.

- **Lakes Regional Park** has 2 great playgrounds, 2 splash pads, a miniature train that will take you on a tour of part of the park, and numerous nature paths that surround a large lake for kayaking. It is also a venue for festivals and concerts.

- **Wa-Ke Hatchee Park and Recreation Center** lets you enjoy yoga, pickle ball, playground, dog park, tennis courts, basketball courts - you name it this rec center has it.

- **Rutenberg Community Park** is one of my favorite summer playgrounds that has huge trees that create a great shaded playground. It's a great way to beat the summer heat.

- **Four Freedoms Park and Recreation Center** has a shaded playground area and multipurpose facility that accommodates activities for Cape Coral residents of all ages.

- **Koreshan State Park** (est. 1894) is home to some of the area's most historic buildings. Originally settled by a group known at the Koreshan Unity, they believed the entire universe existed within the "globe" called planet earth. Nestled along the Estero River on US 41 in Estero, it offers playgrounds, camping, boat ramp, kayaking, fishing, hiking, and picnicking.

- **Ding Darling Wildlife Refuge** on Sanibel has over 220 species of birds. Offers kayak launching sites, biking, and nature hikes.

WATER HAZARDS:
Beware of water hazards like alligators, snakes, and sharks. Freshwater/brackish ponds and lakes can be inhabited by alligators and/or poisonous snakes, so be aware of your surroundings and make sure to not leave food outside that lets animals to equate humans with being fed. Make sure to keep small pets and children away from fresh water. In saltwater I like to think like a fisherman., I tend to stay out of the water when it is dawn or dusk (when fish are feeding) and I also do not swim in passes where you will find a lot of fishermen. Like most animals, in nature they are more afraid of you than you are of them, but I certainly do not want to make it hard for them to tell the difference between me and their meal.

I consider myself a nature lover. In the 30 plus years of living in Southwest Florida, I have hiked miles of trail heads, canoed and swam in freshwater lakes, swam in the open waters of the Gulf of Mexico, and even camped out in the Everglades. I've seen all types of wildlife and have had only had good encounters. I credit understanding the hazards to staying safe when exploring our nature.

Outdoor Fitness

Outdoor fitness activities are bountiful because of our year-round beautiful weather. The sunshine attracts those wanting an active lifestyle and our community is full of clubs to support those interested. A quick search on the internet will yield dozens of clubs for cyclist, swimmers, runners, and other fitness-based clubs. Lee County is dedicated to improving our roads and streets to accommodate pedestrians, runners, and cyclists. Visit www.bikewalklee.org and follow their blog to get up to date maps and events in our area. One of my favorite places to bike is on Sanibel. The City of Sanibel was elevated to "Silver" status Bicycle Friendly Community^{SM} by the League of American Bicyclists. There bike paths and natural beauty make this place a must ride destination!

On the Water

Our county is the fourth in the State of Florida for the number of registered boats. Boaters flock to the Lee Island Coast to take advantage of our beautiful waterways. The Caloosahatchee River, Hendry Creek, Cape Coral Canals System, 10 Mile Canal, Orange River in Fort Myers, the Imperial River in Bonita Springs, and the Estero River in Estero are some of the larger rivers and streams. The vast amount of waterfront properties is why Southwest Florida attracts so many boaters.

Boating

Family Sailboat Fun

Fishing boats and sailboats are the most popular boats you will see in Southwest Florida waters. You'll also find large yachts, small flats boats, pontoon boats, and even off shore racing boats. The Lee County Waterways (www.leewaterways.com) has created a great website with information on local waterways, public boat ramps, tides, fish identification, boating and water safety. It also provides links to other websites which can give you additional information about water temps, water quality, waves, and weather.

Buying vs Renting a Boat

As you can imagine, being surrounded by so much water, you'll find the urge to go out and buy a boat right away is HUGE. I would suggest renting various boats first to see which would work best for you. Boating clubs like Freedom Boat Club and Carefree Boat Club make this easy. Consider these questions: Will you be trailering the boat to water or do you have waterfront property? Check with your Realtor to ensure that the boat you intend to dock at your new house has adequate access. Canal depths, bridges, conditions of waterways may impact the type of boat you can dock behind your home. Be sure to visit the Fort Myers Boat Show to see what is on offer. Additional resources about boat ownership can be found at the SWFL Marine Industries Association (www.swfmia.com).

Fishing/Hunting

The history of fishing goes back 1700 years to the Calusa Indians who lived off the seafood harvested from the Gulf waters. Big fish still swim in these waters by the thousands. You can pick up all your required licensing and read the rules of hunting and fishing for our area at the Florida Fish and Wildlife Conservation Commission website, www. gooutdoorsflorida.com. Licensing costs between $28.00 for a lobster license to $110.50 for a complete hunter's license.

Scuba Diving

The coast of Southwest Florida is home to 20 artificial reefs, 5 of them are sunken ships. The rest have been created over the last 60 years from cars, barges, bridges, and other construction building materials that provide a place for a flourishing reef to grow and for scuba divers to explore. Visit www.eereefs.org for resources about our thriving reef habitat.

Kayaking and More

Follow the path that the Calusa Indians would have taken. The 190 miles of the Great Calusa Blueway is great for paddling. Additionally, you can waterski, windsurf, standup paddle board, and scuba dive. Exploring the waterways will offer you an up-close look at what old Florida used to look like along with a great workout.

Lee County Sports

Lee County Florida has long been a "sports-friendly" destination for many sports, but most notably baseball. Young and old sports fans will have a full schedule from all the games and practices ranging from not only baseball but also sports like basketball, hockey, tennis, and golf.

Baseball

JetBlue Park

The Florida Grapefruit League (www.floridagrapefruitleague.com) heats up in March when Major League preseason games start up. The Boston Red Sox call JetBlue "Fenway South" Stadium home during the winter. The stadium is located on Daniels east of I-75. The Fort Myers Miracle along with Minnesota Twins play at the Hammond Stadium that is located at Six Mile Cypress and Daniels. Spring season game tickets go on sale in early December. Ticket prices range for $9 to $49, so to get a seat, make sure you buy early!

Fenway South at JetBlue Park

http://boston.redsox.mlb.com/bos/spring_training/ballpark
11500 Fenway South Drive
Fort Myers, FL 33913

Hammond Stadium at CenturyLink Sports Complex

http://minnesota.twins.mlb.com/min/spring_training
14100 Six Mile Cypress Parkway
Fort Myers, FL 33912

If you live close to the stadiums, most games start at 1:05pm. Traffic might be heavy during these times and you may want to seek another route.

Hockey and Ice Skating

Florida Everblades was founded in 1998 and plays at the Germain Arena and are a part of the Eastern Conference in the ECHL. The arena is also used as an ice skating, hockey practice, and entertainment venue for large concerts like Elton John, Brad Paisley, Cher, Tom Petty, Zac Brown Band, Cirque du Soleil, and WWE. Also, family events like Disney on Ice, Sesame Street Live, and Wiggles. Check for upcoming events here: www.germainarena.com.

Basketball

Florida Gulf Coast University put Fort Myers on the map nationally when they made it to the Sweet 16 as a 15 seeded NCAA Men's Basketball Team. The press dubbed the team "Dunk City" and they also won an ESPN Espy award for "Best Upset Win". You can find game times online at www.fgcu.edu.

Golf

Southwest Florida has more than 130 public and private golf courses of various skill levels that will keep golfers from beginner to champion busy all year long. Prices range between $20 to $200 per round and during the summer months many private courses are opened to the public. Some courses offer a summer discount. Our beautiful weather and professionally designed courses have attracted major tournaments. That's also why many professional golfers make this area their home.

If living in a golf community is important to you, make sure to work with a Realtor® that specializes in golf course communities. There are many options to consider like:

- What are the membership fees?

- Is there a membership cap?

- Is it a private or public course?

- Are there reciprocal agreements with neighboring communities?

- How busy the courses become during season?

- Where the home is located on the hole?

Having the answers to these and other questions will help you make the best home buying decision.

Exploring

There is so much to do here that it is best to just give you a MUST DO list of favorites! Some of these are easy day trips. And some should be considered a staycation to get the most out of it!

My Favorite Local Activities List

- Lounging on the Lazy River at Sun Splash Waterpark in Cape Coral

- Overnight camping trip in the rustic cottages on the island of Cayo Costa

- Driving down McGregor Boulevard to view homes decorated with Christmas lights and ending up at one of the top 10 historic homes for the holidays - Edison & Ford Winter Estates

- Walk around Sanibel Historical Museum and Village and a stop at the Bailey-Matthew National Shell Museum to see the best shell collection in the world.

- Go out on a deep-sea fishing charter from Fort Myers Beach

- Take the kids on a Pieces of Eight Pirate Cruise

- Enroll the kids in Sanibel Sea Day School while you hit the beach for some R&R

- Calusa Nature Center is a great place to explore as it has 3 nature trails, a museum, a planetarium, butterfly and bird aviary, gift shop, and picnic areas. They also host a haunted night walk during Halloween - it is super scary!

- The Shell Factory in North Fort Myers has it all—mini golf, zip lining, bumper-paddle boats, game room, nature park, along with a petting feeding area, live music, bar, restaurant, and several museum collections.

- In February go on a photographic birding bus tour during the annual burrowing owl festival.

- Keep your eyes to the sky to enjoy the Florida International Air Show at Punta Gorda Airport, named one of the "10 best air shows in the world"

- Daytrip to Key West for a cocktail or two on the Key West Express.

- Try your luck at the Seminole Indian Casino in Immokalee

- Stroll and dine at Fisherman's Village in Punta Gorda

- Glide through mazes of seagrass on an airboat tour in the Everglades National Park

There's still more to do and see in Lee County! Let's take it indoors for some shopping and dining.

CHAPTER 5

THE ART OF SHOPPING, DINING, AND ENTERTAINMENT

One benefit of our tourism industry comes in the form of our dining, shopping, arts, and entertainment options. You will find that our residents come from all corners of the world and with them they bring a variety of fashions, flavors, styles, sights, and sounds to stimulate all your senses! Let's first introduce you to the style of home furnishings.

Home Furnishing Styles

Out With The Old And In With The New
by Ruth Condit

Thirteen years ago, fresh from selling our Pennsylvania home, my husband and I launched a ten-day house hunt in Southwest Florida. I learned one thing from the marathon viewings. Antiques and reproductions of the dark wood 18th and 19th century variety, heavy curtains and orientals do not look good in Florida. Many homes up for sale had crowded interiors transported directly from the owner's northern or midwest residence. Scarsdale in the subtropics. Out of touch, out of place.

Florida is sunny and bright and hot. Casual is key in interiors... be it of the country club kind or the beach kind. If you can, take some time to get a feel for what Florida homes ask for and want to be. Visit high-end models and condominiums, showrooms at Estero's Miromar Design Center and the many fine furniture stores lining Route 41 from South Fort Myers to Naples. Browse the local design magazines devoted to luxury interiors created in our area.

Fortunately, most of todays' hot trends work here: painted finishes, reclaimed wood, bold overscale prints, mixed prints, shots of bright accent colors, pale colors, and plantation shutters always with or without stationary window panels on either side. And no design advice is complete without mentioning the classic, tried and true blue and white color scheme. Pair it with beige, yellow, pink, plum, lime green or orange...the list is limitless and looks right.

If Lee County is to be your primary residence, sell what you don't want in your home state. You will get a much better price. Also, chances are your move is a downsizing. What a wonderful opportunity to change your style and decorate against type. Traditional up there? Buy modern down here. Liked white or beige up there, go bright and bold down here. New home. New you.

"But what about my precious family heirlooms?" you ask. Bring them. But mix them judiciously with your new purchases. They will add character and interest. Reupholster period pieces in unexpected colors. Choose Indoor-outdoor fabrics to use white without worry. Turn your old books around: spines back, pages front. Display your vintage accessories as pieces of sculpture.

You may, after reading this, feel a bit overwhelmed. Let a design professional help you with the planning. If you are a do-it-yourselfer, arrange a one or two hour consultation for direction and ideas. For more extensive assistance, you can work with a designer from floor plan to finished project. Whatever you decide, have fun, shed the old and embrace the new!

Ruth Condit holds a Fine Arts BA and Certificate in Interior Design from the prestigious New York School of Interior Design. Ruth Condit Interiors Contact: (239) 462-3328 www.ruthconditinteriors.com

Fashion Clothing Trends

Southwest Florida has become a destination for smart shoppers. Our large outlet centers draw in cost conscious fashionistas from all over the world to get the latest styles at the lowest prices. A variety of fashion trends are available in the Fort Myers area by the top designers. You will notice that most residents dress on the casual side weather they are going to work, to school, to the beach, and even to church. It's not uncommon to see people wearing sandals or fancy flip flops to just about anywhere.

When packing for your move to the sunshine state you will not need to pack up your heavy winter items. Think minimalism. Sell them, donate them or give them to your friends to remember you by, because you will not need them anymore!

Clothing Capsule: Capsule Wardrobes have been around for years and have made a resurgence lately as people move to embrace the minimalistic movement. Moving to a warmer climate is a great time to shed the quantity of clothes you have and focus on the quality of cloths. Consider your lifestyle and clothing needs and then try to choose 40 pieces that can move with you. Free yourself of the old and move down with the clothes you love.

Once you have settled in, check out my favorite shopping hubs to add to your clothing wardrobe capsule:

- **Coconut Point (R)** (www.simon.com/mall/coconut-point) is a sprawling outdoor resort like shopping center that has everything you could want from over 140 stores that include Target, Dillards, Regal Movie Theater, Apple, Michael Kors, Barnes and Noble to name a few. There are many delicious dining options and Fashion Drive also has condos you can live in above the stores.

- **Miromar Outlets** (http://www.miromaroutlets.com) is my favorite outlet shopping destination - it has over 140 store including Saks Fifth Avenue OFF 5th, Neiman Marcus Last Call, Bloomingdale's Outlet. In addition to the shopping, you can join one of several fitness groups like Fitness Camp or Baby Boot Camp and enjoy the beautiful fountains and walkways. Live entertainment is also offered along with a covered playground for kids.

- **Gulf Coast Town Center** (www.gulfcoasttowncenter.com) is also a large outdoor mall with Target, Belk, JC Penney, Bass Pro Shops, Regal Movie Theater, and Costco as its main anchor stores. There are also many restaurants to choose from. Other shops include Ross, Jo Ann, HomeGoods, and Dick's Sporting Goods.

- **Bell Tower Shops** (www.thebelltowershops.com) is a pet loving outdoor shopping mall that has been recently remodeled to host live music venues in the center square. In addition to several dining options and fashion forward stores like Talbots, Chico's, and White House Black Market, you will find Bed, Bath, and Beyond, Ulta, a 20-plex Stadium Movie Theater, and a gourmet grocer called Fresh Market.

- **Sanibel Outlets** (www.sanibeloutlets.com) is a smaller outlet mall with a coffee shop and small playground, but one worth visiting. Make sure you pick up a free coupon book at the mall office before shopping for additional savings.

- **Edison Mall** (www.shopedisonmall.com) is a traditional mall with inside walkways with 127 specialty stores, lots of food court choices, and four main anchor store: Sears, JCPenney's, Dillard's, and Macy's.

As you can see fashion and food go hand and hand at our shopping centers. There are delicious dishes all over Southwest Florida to be found and Sarah E. Crain, author of **Bucket List for Foodies,** can give you the 411 on the first 50 dishes you have to eat!

Bucket List for Foodies

By Sarah E. Crain
Author Of Bucket List For Foodies For Southwest Florida

Food Festivals

Southwest Florida has a "fest" for just about every type of food, one of the largest is the Taste of the Town at Jet Blue Park also known as Fenway South. It is put on by the very active Junior League of Fort Myers (jlfm.org). It is a great place to find your new favorite dishes all in one location and it's a charity event as well, so you can feel the love as you spend and eat for a good cause. Other fun food fests to take a bite out of are:

- Bacon Fest www.ftmyersbeerandbacon.com
- Mango Fest www.mangomaniafl.net
- Shrimp Fest www.fortmyersbeachshrimpfestival.com
- Taps & Tunes Fest www.sbdac.com/event/tapsandtunes
- Oktoberfest www.capecoraloktoberfest.com
- Greek Fest www.greekfestfortmyers.com
- Stone Crab Fest www.stonecrabfestival.org
- Coconut Festival www.cocofest.com
- Taste of the Islands, which benefits CROW www.crowclinic.org
- Taste of Lee www.tasteoflee.com

Residents not only have an appetite for good food, but also good spirits. Craft beers from a variety of local brew houses should be on your list of things to try: Fat Point Brewing, Fort Myers Brewing Co., Momentum Brewhouse, Millennial Brewing Company, Old Soul Brewery, and Point Ybel Brewing Company. If beer is not your thing, Cape Coral is home to Wicked Dolphin Artisan Rum (www.wickeddolphinrum.com), a rum distillery that offers free tours and tastings.

Grocery Stores

Young Family Shopping at Fresh Market

Publix Super Markets www.publix.com has more than 30 stores in Lee County and is probably the most beloved grocer in all of Florida. They offer Boars Head brand meats and cheeses in their deli department, together with tasty sandwich rolls to make the world's best subs. Their bakery has exquisite cakes and cupcakes with buttercream frosting. Upon leaving you will be assisted by a fine lady or gentleman that helps you out to your car to load your groceries and then bring back the carts (no rogue carts flying through the parking lot here). Publix is so friendly you will truly understand why their motto is "Where shopping is a pleasure".

We have several Winn Dixie Grocery www.winndixie.com stores that offer great deals on a variety of items every week. Budget minded shoppers will love Winn Dixie's customer reward card for weekly special deals.

Fresh Market has two locations—one in Bell Tower in Fort Myers and one in Bonita Springs. (https://www.thefreshmarket.com)

You'll find Ada's Natural Market on College Parkway in Fort Myers (https://adasmarket.com)

Coming soon is a Whole Foods at Daniels and Six Mile Cypress. Locals can't wait for this newest addition to the healthy food movement.

We have several Walmart Super Stores www.walmart.com and also a Walmart Neighborhood Market, which is the smaller sibling to the Walmart Superstore. Both stores are open 24 hours a day. This is great if you find yourself out of something important when typical stores would be closed.

Chances are no matter what corner of Lee County you choose to make your home; you will have a Wholesale Club nearby. Sam's Club (www.samsclub.com), BJ's, (www.bjs.com), and Costco (www.costco.com) are the three main wholesale clubs. My personal favorite has been Costco, because it is close to home and carries many organic items.

Ethnic Food and Fresh Farmers Markets

Southwest Florida residents come from all over the world and thankfully they have brought their taste buds with them. The demand for ethnic grocers risen over the years and created a burgeoning sector of ethnic food markets that I have had the joy of uncovering. Indian Markets, Asian Markets, Latino Markets, Italian Markets and farmer's markets make it easy to eat healthy flavorful foods all year round. One favorite is Lakes Park Farmers Market (www.buylocallee.com)

Arts and Entertainment

Now that you have filled your home, pantry, and closet with all that Southwest Florida has to offer food, fashion, and style wise, it is time to hit the arts and entertainment scene. The arts and entertainments venues is a great way to get social and meet some new friends!

Visual Arts Scene

When the weather is oppressive for those up north, artists from across the country load up their artwork and head south for what I like to call, "The Great Art Migration". Practically every week of the winter you can find an art festival somewhere in Florida. Art mediums from ceramic, glass, wood, metal, sculpture, digital photography and graphics, drawings and paintings in pastels, acrylics, watercolors, wearable woven pieces and jewelry can be found traveling from town to town in sunny and breezy outdoor art festivals. It is one of my favorite ways to find new and interesting artists from all over the world.

A Festive Evening at ArtFest. Courtesy: Prima Luce

Artfest of Fort Myers (www.artfestfortmyers.com) and Cape Coral Festival of Arts (www.capecoralfestival.com) are the two largest festivals with hundreds of artists and 100,000 people visiting each year. Check their websites for dates and vendor information.

ALLIANCE OF THE ARTS LIVE, WORK, & PLAY IN LEE.

By Lydia Black

Southwest Florida's art offerings are as diverse as the region's flora and fauna. From the Fort Myers stage of the Florida Repertory Theatre to the galleries at BIG Arts on Sanibel Island, visitors and residents have a breadth of cultural offerings to choose from each and every day. We have access to world-class music, dance, theater, culinary, literary, film and visual arts.

This access is important, as we believe that the arts are truly essential to the health and vitality of our SWFL communities. They remind us to slow down, be mindful and connect more truly with what's really important. They enhance our quality of life and play an instrumental role in educating a new generation of dynamic thinkers. What might not be so obvious is the fact that our galleries, theaters, performance halls and art-centric organizations form a real growth industry that creates and supports jobs, generates revenue, attracts businesses and residents, and acts as a cornerstone for cultural tourism.

Our vibrant and strong artistic community makes SWFL a great place to LIVE, WORK and PLAY. Come dance, draw, drum, sculpt, write, paint, or play and enhance your quality of life and the lives of everyone around you. Take advantage of downtown Fort Myers' monthly ArtWalk & MusicWalk, catch a show at the Barbara B. Mann Preforming Arts Hall or visit one of the many art festivals produced in our area. You won't be sorry you did.

Lydia Antunes Black is the Executive Director of the Alliance for the Arts - the officially designated Arts organization for Lee County which is responsible for Connecting Art, Culture & Community. For information about the Alliance visit www.artinlee.org or contact us at 239-939-2787.

As Lydia pointed out, there are a number of art galleries for you to tap into within the arts community. Here is an extensive list of organizations that help make our area such a great place to live in:

- Alliance for the Arts www.artinlee.org

- DAAS Co-op Art Gallery and Gifts www.daascoop.com

- Arts for ACT Gallery www.artsforactgallery.com

- Space 39 Modern Art www.spacethirtynine.com

- Cape Coral Art League www.capecoralartleague.org

- Fort Myers Art League www.artleagueoffortmyers.org

- Coconut Pointe Gallery www.acswf.org

- BIG Arts Sanibel Island www.bigarts.org

- FSW Rauschenberger Gallery www.rauschenberggallery.com

- FGCU art Galleries
  www.artgallery.fgcu.edu/FGCU_Art_Galleries.html

- Gannon's Antiques & Art Gallery
  www.gannonsantiques.com

- Artis-Naples www.artisnaples.org (further south, but worth the trip)

- Wild Child Art Gallery (Matlacha)
  www.wildchildartgallery.com

- Lovegrove Gallery & Gardens (Matlacha)
  www.leomalovegrove.com

If you are feeling creative, local artists teach a variety of classes at some of the community art galleries listed above. You can "Live, Work, and Play" in Lee County.

Performing and Music Arts Scene

Big name stars like Elton John, Amy Schumer, Brad Paisley, Zac Brown and Josh Grobin have played at Germain Arena located in Estero. This venue can host an audience of up to 8000 people which has brought an impressive list of sold out shows. Barbara B. Mann Performing Arts Hall, which is named after one of the pioneers in the Fort Myers Arts Scene, seats 1871 people. A number of spectacular Broadway Series shows and entertainers have taken the stage over the last 30 years to entertain our residents and visitors. Big names like Tony Bennett, Bill Crystal, Jerry Seinfeld, Alton Brown, and productions like Cinderella, Annie, Phantom of the Opera, Chicago, and the Nutcracker are a few of my favorites.

The Florida Repertory Theater

More intimate performance settings can be found throughout Southwest Florida at venues like Royal Palm Dinner Theatre (www. broadwaypalm.com), the Seminole Murder Mystery Dinner Train (www.semgulf.com), and the Florida Repertory (www.floridarep. org) which performs shows in the downtown historic Arcade Theatre. The Fort Myers Film Festival (www.fortmyersfilmfestival.com), along with the Southwest Florida Symphony (www.swflso.org) and Gulf Coast Symphony, (www.gulfcoastsymphony.org) are also popular entertainment options .The Island Hopper Songwriter festival brings some incredibly talented songwriters to Southwest Florida that happens in 3 locations over a two week time period across Lee County.

The Sidney & Berne Davis Art Center (www.sbdac.com) is now housed in the old Fort Myers post office that was almost entirely rehabbed. One of the most unusual visual art pieces you will find downtown is the Caloosahatchee Manuscripts. This art installation was donated by Florida Power and Light in 1998 to commemorate the switch from using oil to natural gas. Sculptor Jim Sunborn was commissioned to create the two light sculptures. The western drum outlines the Latin names of plants that Edison tested in his labs for his inventions, while the eastern one tells a story of native American Indians' migration which ties into the historic symbolism of the site. Sanborn used a Creek/Seminole legend since there is no Calusa written text. Source: http://www.artswfl.com/public-art-2/fort-myers-river-district-public-art-2/caloosahatchee-manuscripts/caloosahatchee-manuscripts

Literary Arts

The Southwest Florida Reading Festival is celebrated every March. Multiple stages are set up so popular authors can have readings, meet and greets with fans at the Harborside Event Center. For the kids, several storytelling areas and a craft tent are set up and kids are given FREE books to take home, too! You can download the "Readfest" App for iOS or Android to make your visit a breeze. Support literacy in Lee County by attending "Read between the Wines," a Chocolate & Spirits Festival that raises money for the reading festival. For more information visit www.readfest.org.

Entertainment

First Street Dining Downtown Courtesy: Prima Luce

Fort Myers is not your traditional nightclub laden city. Although you can find a few wild party spots, most people young and old prefer to relax and relish the good life with minimum stress and drama. Six Bends™ Harley-Davidson ® is like an amusement park for adults who love to ride. Check out their calendar of events. You never know what they have put together.

Downtown also has an impressive selection of bars and restaurants. The Standard is anything but standard. The historic Veranda will take you back to the roots of Fort Myers. Ford's Garage, Cabos, Firestones, and Capone's serve up fun times and great food and drink. Make sure to seek out unique smaller dining establishments like Bruno's of Brooklyn, Untied Bistro, Twisted Vine, and Blu Sushi.

Enjoy the sun setting over the Caloosahatchee while listening to music and sipping cocktails at the Martini Bar and Sky bar or the Hotel Indigo Roof Top Bar. After the sun sets, the pubs and clubs star to heat up. Visit the Celsius, City Tavern, and the Lodge to keep the good time flowing.

Southwest Florida covers a large area and there is a plethora of cultural and art related activities for you to enjoy and become involved in. I encourage you to subscribe to the community calendars and follow socially on Facebook or other social media outlet for the activities that interest you most.

Event Calendars

How can you possibly take part in all these activities? The best way is to subscribe to one of these active online calendars to stay current on what is happening in Lee County. Check these listed below monthly to ensure you don't miss special events, activities, and festivals:

- Fort Myers Florida Weekly (www.Floridaweekly.com)

- Sanibel & Captiva Events (www.sanibel-island.sanibel-captiva.org/events)

- Fort Myers Beach News & Events (www.IslandSandPaper.com)

- Fort Myers Beach "The Catch" (www.fortmyersbeach.org)

- Fort Myers River District (www.myriverdistrict.com/events)

- Gulf Coast Times (www.gulfcoasttimes.net)

- Arts & Entertainment Happenings (www.happeningsmagazine.net) distributed to over 500 locations around Southwest Florida.

- Got Kids? Subscribe to HulaFrog and get weekly or daily email updates of family friendly events. www.hulafrog.com/fort-myers-fl.

Historic Downtown Fort Myers hosts many events each month. My favorites are Art Walk, Music Walk, and Mystery Walk. Follow the River District Alliance | Fort Myers Florida website for updated information on events.

Top 12 Events Of The Year By Month
Mark Your Calendar

January: Taps & Tunes Craft Beer/Music Festival (Downtown)

February: Edison Festival of Lights (Downtown)

March: Southwest Florida Reading Festival (Downtown)

April: Cardboard Boat Regatta (Cape Coral)

May: Taste of Fort Myers Beach (Fort Myers Beach)

June: Rodeo & Reggae Party Fishing Tournament (Fort Myers Beach)

July: Mango Mania Harvest Festival (Pine Island)

August: Bucklers Craft Fair (Fort Myers)

September: Island Hopper Songwriter Festival (Fort Myers, Fort Myers Beach, and Captiva)

October: Octoberfest Cape Coral German American Club

November: Largest American Sand-Sculpting Competition (Fort Myers Beach)

December: Luminary Festival (Sanibel Captiva)

CHAPTER 6

CAN YOU LIVE WELL IN LEE COUNTY?

Cost of Living

Fort Myers has a lower cost of living than the US average, reports Sperling's Best Places in it's most recent report. Visit BestPlaces.com to see the cost of living compared to your hometown. This will give you an idea of how to best prepare financially for your move to the Fort Myers area. Grocery and transportation costs are higher than the national average, so consider budgeting in those areas to keep costs down.

Housing costs can vary street by street, even house by house in Southwest Florida. Finding an experienced licensed local realtor, lender or rental agent is the best way for you to find the right location and home while keeping the costs within your budget.

Affordable housing can be found throughout Lee County. Down payment and closing cost assistance programs like the Local Housing Assistance Plan, HOME Down Payment Assistance Program, Florida Bond Program, Neighborhood Stabilization Program, and Community Workforce Housing Innovation Pilot Program can work in conjunctions with loan programs like USDA, FHA, and VA loans to make homeownership a reality. View the Realtor® Association of Great Fort Myers and the Beaches website for in-depth information (www.greaterftmyers.com).

Affordable housing is not just limited to buying a home. You can also rent affordably, too. It is a good idea to plan ahead if you think you may be moving to Fort Myers, many of the lower cost rental communities have waitlists. You can search for affordable rental options here: www.floridahousingsearch.org, www.roommates.com, and www.florida.sublet.com.

Utilities

The utility services offered vary based on the location, construction, and age of your home. Below you will find all the utility options available throughout Lee County that will keep you cool in the summer, warm in the winter, entertained, and connected to the world 365 days a year.

Lee County Electrical Coop (800) 599-2356 Covers Cape Coral, Pine Island, Captiva, Sanibel, North Fort Myers, and parts of Lehigh Acres. LCEC also offers a budgeting online program called KILOwatch. It allows you to set up alerts when you reach certain usage limits. It's a great way to keep your electric budget in check during the summer months.

Florida Power & Light (239) 334-7754 Covers the rest of Lee County extending from Alva, Gateway, Estero, Bonita Springs, Fort Myers Beach, Iona, and Fort Myers. Their website will allow you to manage your accounts and take advantage of their budget billing that will let you pay the average monthly bill over 12 months.

Rebates, discounts and more... Once you are in your home, make sure you visit your power company's website and sign up for energy tips. Over the years our electric companies along with the state of Florida have offered rebates for things like new air conditioning units, duct replacement, and solar powered hot water heaters. Keeping in contact with your power company could save you money down the line. You can also manage your account, report power outages, request tree trimming, and have an energy survey completed to find ways to lower your homes electric bill.

Teco Peoples Gas (877) 832-6747 Some of the newer SWFL Communities have been built with natural gas access installed. These include Belle Lago, Coastal Key, Pelican Preserve, Bonita Lakes, The Brooks, Villas Palmeras, Estero Place, and the Reserve at Estero. You can find homes for sale in Zillow by searching "Fort Myers Homes with Gas".

Solar Systems - We are in the sunshine state, so you will find several options of installing a house-wide solar system. This is called a photo voltaic solar system. You will still to be connected to the power grid through one of power companies above. But taking advantage of the average 266 days of sunshine Fort Myers can possibly save you some money in the long term.

Florida Flood, Homeowners, Auto, and Rental
by Brian Culbertson

Did you know that Fort Myers is one of the flattest cities in the country? While flooding rarely happens, it's still a good idea to make sure that you're covered in case of a flood. Fort Myers is a coastal community, so we get to enjoy the sunshine and being on the water frequently, but it also means—on rare occasion—that water could end up in your house. Insurance to cover this risk is not typically provided in a homeowner's policy, so it must be purchased separately.

Congress created the National Flood Insurance Program in 1968 and requires owners of mortgaged property in what are called Special Flood Hazard Areas to carry flood insurance. FEMA produces Flood Insurance Rate Maps (FIRM's) to determine these Special Flood Hazard Areas and Lee County issues a Flood Insurance Rate Map to keep everyone updated on the rates for their areas.

Assuming that the topography of Lee County won't change for a while, I'll tell you that about half of Fort Myers is zoned as being subject to inundation by 1% annual chance of shallow flooding. This means that expected flooding in that 1% chance may have average depths between one and three feet. The other half—the areas more inland—are about 0.2% annual chance of flooding (0.2% translates to about once every 500 years).

The biggest threat to flooding in Fort Myers comes from hurricanes with a storm surge. Thankfully, major hurricanes (ones with wind speeds of 200mph and above) only make landfall about once every 15 to 30 years. A storm surge is what happens with a low-pressure weather event—like a hurricane—acts like a giant vacuum and raises the sea level directly under it by several feet. It's far from a tsunami, but it'll dump a ton of water in your backyard if you live along the coast.

As far as what you can do to save money on your flood insurance, the best thing you can do is elevate the base of your house. For new construction homes, this means building the foundation above your community's base flood elevation. For example, a home with its first floor elevated 1 foot above the base flood elevation can result in an annual flood premium reduction of about 30%.

On the topic of saving money on homeowner's insurance, one thing to consider is that you can switch from replacement cost on your personal property to actual cash value. Actual cash value is the replacement cost minus depreciation, so it's like receiving garage sale prices on your property. Keep in mind though that actual cash value may not completely cover your property since it factors in depreciation; so speak with an agent about your options.

One more piece of advice: you may want to raise your wind deductible within your homeowner's policy. Deductibles for wind coverage can range from 1% of the insured value, all the way up to 10% of the insured value. The thing to remember is that this percentage deductible is from the insured value, not from the percentage of the claim. Check your risk tolerance before making this change as it could result in a significant rate decrease.

Brian Culbertson
Culbertson Agency
www.culbertsonagency.com
(239) 210-7700

Healthcare

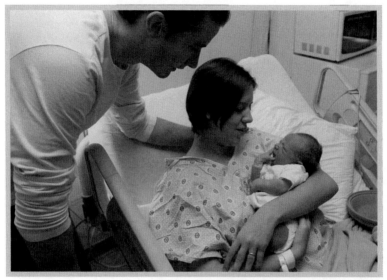

Mom and Dad Welcome Their Newborn Baby

Lee Health Systems cared for its first patient Sam Thompson for appendicitis in 1916. As they celebrate more than 100 years of service to our community, Lee County benefits from an award-winning healthcare system helping over a million patients each year. Lee Memorial has more than 13,000 employees and 4,000 volunteers and is the largest public health system in the state that receives no direct tax support.

Navigating Lee County Health Care
by Dr. Suzanne Felt

Welcome to Lee County! You are lucky enough to be in a county with an award winning comprehensive health care system. The Lee Health System is the primary health care system in Lee County. It is comprised of four acute care hospitalists. Although every hospital can accommodate most patients each hospital has specialized departments and care services that are unique to it. As a new resident of Lee County, we want to help you find your way to the facility that best accommodates your needs.

Let's start with establishing yourself or your family with a primary care doctor. This is a task best accomplished even before you make the move to Lee County. It will keep you out of the dangerous gap of going without doctors during your transition or while you are here for the winter.

If you find yourself in need of urgent healthcare services, you will be relieved to know you have a wide range of options here in Lee County. First, if time permits, always check-in with your primary care doctor about your acute symptoms. Often, an appointment can be scheduled to discuss the urgent symptoms and it's always a good idea discuss your medical needs with your personal family physician. Please familiarize yourself with where your doctors or specialists practice. Often different specialty groups have a preferred hospital campus.

Another great option for acute care is our expansive urgent care system. In addition to many private urgent care centers; Lee Convenient Care offers convenient walk-in medical services for minor emergencies and illnesses 7am-7pm seven days per week (times differ per facility).

There are four acute care hospitals within Lee Health, each with a fully functional Emergency Department to meet your highest emergency care needs. Selecting the correct facility is critically important because each hospital has unique specialty services.

For example:

- Golisano Children's Hospital located at Healthpark Medical Center is your best bet for pediatric care.

- Lee Memorial Hospital in downtown Fort Myers has no obstetric services but has the areas only level II trauma center.

- There are 2 operational cardiac catheratizion labs at Gulf Coast Hospital and Health Park Medical Center.

- Each hospital has a unique niche and familiarizing yourself with these specialties will help you get the best care possible.

Finally, the emergency department services of Lee County provide exemplary lifesaving care, but often during the heavy tourism months (Jan-May) there can be a significant wait time and delays in services. If the roads, restaurants and beaches are busy, so is the hospital waiting room!! Seeking out care from your family doctor, using convenient care as an alternative, and selecting the correct hospital facility will ensure that you get the most prompt compassionate care possible.

ABOUT DR. SUZANNE FELT: Dr. Suzanne Felt is a board-certified Emergency Medicine Physician at Lee Memorial Hospital. Suzanne along with her husband, also a practicing physician, and their daughter make their home in Fort Myers. Together they enjoy exploring the great outdoor adventures SWFL has to offer. They have been featured on Season 9 of the hit TV show "Untold Stories of the ER."

Gulf Coast Medical Center

There are several award-winning hospitals within the Lee Health System. Healthgrades® looks at three key factors to help provide patients with transparency when choosing a healthcare facility. These three factors are patient satisfaction, experience match, and hospital quality. You can find more information about the Lee Health System hospitals at www.leehealth.org.

- Gulf Coast Medical Center is a highly rated hospital with 349 beds. Its major service lines are neuroscience and the Neuroscience Institute, orthopedics, and general surgery. In fact, Gulf Coast Medical Center is an accredited Comprehensive Stroke Center and has the physician coverage and technology to treat all stroke patients, including bleeding strokes—such as those caused by brain aneurysms. The hospital houses the region's only Kidney Transplant Center. The spacious emergency department consists of 28 exam rooms, 10 observation units, and 33 treatment rooms. It has received 12 Healthgrades 5-star ratings and 2 Quality awards.

- Lee Memorial Hospital is a 355-bed acute care facility and is the flagship hospital for Lee Health. The hospital has received the 2018 Distinguished Hospital Award for Clinical Excellence™. It offers a Level II Trauma Center, servicing Lee county and the surrounding areas. The hospital has one of the top 10 most active joint replacement centers in the U.S., and houses The Rehabilitation Hospital, a 60-bed comprehensive inpatient rehabilitation facility. It serves 50,000 patients annually with a staff of 1000 physicians.

- HealthPark Medical Center is fully accredited through the Society of Chest Pain Centers. They have been awarded 17 Healthgrades® 5-Star Ratings and 5 Healthgrades® Quality Awards in the past year. They provide a broad range of services, including catheterization, diagnostic, endoscopy, cardiac rehabilitation, chest pain center, open heart surgery, obstetrics, gynecology, endovascular surgery, rehabilitation, neuroendovascular surgery, emergency room, and radiology. HealthPark has also been awarded Healthgrades® America's 50 Best Hospitals™ for 2014 and 2015.

- Cape Coral Hospital is fully accredited through the Joint Commission. They have the largest emergency room in Lee County and have 291 private rooms. They have received 10 Healthgrades® 5-Star Ratings in the past year. Medical services provided include accredited primary stroke center, chest pain unit, neurosurgical unit, women's care, family birth suites, special care nursery, cardio/diagnostic cardiac angioplasty, pulmonary critical care specialist, chronic disease programs, endoscopy, gastroenterologist, certified diabetes program, pulmonary/cardiac rehab, lab imagining services, and breast health center.

- Golisano Children's Hospital of Southwest Florida has 128 pediatric beds and is the only accredited children's hospital between Tampa and Miami. There are over 70 pediatric specialists that operate 19 different specialized children programs including Pediatric and NeoNatal Intensive Care Unit and Pediatric Cancer Care Program just to name a few. For the second year in a row they have been awarded the Leapfrog award by the non-profit survey rating company Leapfrog Group.

- Lehigh Acres Medical Center is accredited by The Joint Commission. It is an 88-bed short term acute care facility that services east Lee County and surrounding communities. Lehigh Regional Sports and Rehab (LSR) along with The Wound Care Center operate adjacent to the Medical Center. You can find more information online at www.lehighregional. com.

- Bonita Community Health Center offers 7-day a week service with no appointment required. Acute medical issues are treated as well as flu, respiratory issues, allergies, lacerations, injuries. Board Certified Physicians have experience in emergency and family medicine and pediatrics. Complete onsite imaging services (X-Ray, MRI, CT Scans, Ultrasounds, Mammograms) for a more thorough evaluation and faster diagnosis.

- Coming in late 2018 is Lee Health's new health and wellness center in Estero. The new facility will include a freestanding ER, an outpatient surgery center, a wellness center and a variety of other clinics.

Physicians' Offices

Our county has an abundance of physician offices ranging from large multi-office facilities to small boutique and homeopathic healthcare options. Visit the physician's website to view physician profiles, summary of services, patient reviews, credentials, locations, availability, and the types of insurance accepted.

Here are a few of the larger well-established practices in Lee County:

Lee Physician Group is part of Lee Health System. They have more than 572 physicians in dozens of office locations throughout Southwest Florida. After hour care is available through their convenient care office. www.leememorial.org/lee-physician-group

Physicians' Primary Care is an independent healthcare facility with 45 physicians covering 5 different specialties: Internal medicine, family practice, obstetrics, gynecology, and pediatrics. They have offices in Fort Myers, Cape Coral, and Lehigh Acres and are open 365 days a year. www.ppcswfl.com

Internal Medicine Associates (IMA) is a multi-specialty physicians group with over 50 providers in 4 locations throughout Lee County. In addition to their family practice, they offer infusion therapy, weight management programs, in-house laboratory, physical therapy, radiology, and sleep studies. Two EZ-Care Clinics are also available for existing patients. Visit IMA online at www.imadoctors.com for more information.

Other Types of Healthcare

Southwest Florida has a numerous types of healthcare options for its residents. Walk in clinics that are open 7 days a week for minor, non-emergeny illnesses and injuries help ease the burden of emergency rooms, lessening long wait time. You can also visit www.urgentcarelocations.com to get a list of locations.

Family Health Care Centers of Southwest Florida has 21 medical and 8 dental offices that serve Lee, Charlotte, and parts of Hendry Counties. It is one of area's largest comprehensive care providers that offer reduced costs. Visit http://www.fhcswf.org for more information.

Lee County Health Department has Women's Health, Childhood Vaccinations, Women, Infant, Children (WIC) Nutrition Program, Infectious Disease, STD testing, Dental Services, many of which are low cost or free services. Visit http://lee.floridahealth.gov for more details.

Blood Centers

Lee Memorial Health System has 4 blood centers that help maintain the supply needed for the community. Please consider donating at any of the following locations:

- Lee Memorial Hospital

- Summerlin Crossing

- Cape Coral Hospital

- Bonita Community Health Center

- Blood-Mobile (location varies)

The donation center addresses can be found online at www.leememorial.org/bloodcenter or by calling (239) 343-2333.

VA Healthcare Center

The Lee County VA Healthcare Center in Cape Coral was opened in 2012 to replace the VA Outpatient Clinic in Fort Myers that had served the area since 1979. The energy efficient building along with the open floor plan and coffee bistro make it an inviting place for those that have served our country. The 220,000-square foot outpatient facility offers free convenient parking and is one of 8 outpatient clinics operating under the Bay Pines VA Healthcare System, which is headquartered in Bay Pines, Florida, outside of Tampa. You can plan your visit ahead of time online at www.baypines.va.gov.

Healthy Lee County

Business as well as community groups and organizations understand the importance of having healthy residents. Our community has created a coalition called Healthy Lee that provides tools, resources, and programs online to keep Lee County residents focused on continued health. Visit the www.healthylee.com website for more information.

Fire and Safety In Lee County

Fire Department

Lee County has 41 Fire Departments and Fire Stations that are made up of 5 divisions: Fire Prevention, Administration/Operations, Special Services, Training, and Emergency Management. You can visit www.fortmyersfire.com for more information about their services.

Fire Department
2404 Dr. Martin Luther King, Jr. Blvd.
Fort Myers, FL 33901
Ph: 239-321-7311
Fx: 239-334-1625
Emergency: 9-1-1

Fire Prevention
1825 Hendry Street, Suite 101
Fort Myers, FL 33901
Ph: 239-321-7350
Fx: 239-344-5913

Police Departments

When choosing an area to live, consider the safety and security of the area. The Fair Housing Act prohibits Realtors® from answering questions about a neighborhood's safety. It is the buyer's responsibility to do their homework and the Internet makes this very easy to do. Several websites compile data from the area police departments to show an area's relative safety. For example Trulia.com home search website uses both SpotCrime.com and CrimeReports.com to display reported crime information on a google map. In addition, www.

city-data.com/crime will give you geographically referenced crime statistics.

Lee County Sheriff Department services all of Lee County and also have full-service districts that are smaller community based police departments. This allows the Sheriff's Department to make sure they are meeting needs throughout the county. Additionally, the Sheriff's Department has several community-based programs that include: V.O.I.C.E (volunteers and observers that assist deputies), Project Lifesaver, Crime Prevention Programs and Services, and a Youth Explorer Club. www.sheriffleefl.org (239) 477-1000 / Emergency 911

Cape Coral Police Department serves all of Cape Coral. They offer several community programs including Citizens Police Academy, Neighborhood Watch, Police Volunteer Unit, Project Lifesaver, Ride-Alongs, Seniors vs. Crime, and youth/family based activities like Do the Right Thing, Police Explores, and Shop with a Cop. You can visit their website to access their daily bulletin and to view the map to see the location where police reports have been filed.

www.capecops.com (239) 574-3223 / Emergency 911

Fort Myers Police Department services the incorporated areas of Fort Myers. They have a host of programs for our youth like the Explorers Club, KOPS for kids, PAL (a youth sports league), Respect For Law Camp, and Do The Right Thing program that recognize and rewards youths. Additionally adults can get involved with the Citizen Police Academy (CPA), Volunteer In Policing (VIP), Neighborhood Watch and the Annual COPS & Joggers 5K. www.fmpolice.com (239) 321-7000 / Emergency 911

Sanibel Police Department protects and serves the residents, visitors, the eco-system, and the wildlife that inhabit Sanibel Island. In 2018 they were designated as the 7th safest city in the State of Florida, based on an FBI crime statistic report. Captiva Island is considered unincorporated Lee County, which means it falls under the jurisdiction of the Lee County Sheriff Department and also follows the zoning rules for the county. Both departments will serve each other's areas in an emergency situation. Sanibel Police Department also oversees the emergency management plan. The MySanibel.com website has a list of ordinances that pertain to shelling, alligators, bonfires, fireworks, parking rules, and bike safety just to name a few. If you are considering moving or visiting Sanibel, take a moment to familiarize yourself with these ordinances.

Visit the police department website for services, programs, and find answers to questions that may be helpful to keep you and your family safe. Department websites, phone numbers, and addresses can be found in our **Web Links and Extras Section** in the back of this book.

Emergency Management

The Public Safety Department is made up of several divisions and agencies with the goal of keeping Lee County residents and visitors safe. They coordinate the 911 Emergency Dispatch for the county, operate a CodeRED emergency alert program, and have a resource guide to help families prepare for hurricanes and tropical storms. You can sign up for CodeRED emergency alert program and access the resource information on the County's website by visiting: www. leegov.com/publicsafety.

CHAPTER 7

WHAT ARE MY EDUCATION OPTIONS?

Infant and Toddler Care

The Fort Myers area has many types of childcare options available for infant and toddlers. Options include traditional daycare or preschool that are home based and facility based. Many are faith-based programs that are sponsored by local area churches and are open to the public. Additionally, there are several privately owned secular child care programs such as Montessori schools, parent co-ops, along with government assisted programs throughout our county.

Make sure to verify the certification of preschools and daycares before making your decision. There are several approved accrediting agencies that the Florida Department of Children and Families allows to participate in the Gold Seal Quality Care designation program. This accreditation requires providers to maintain higher education standards for children, with a goal of making them better prepared for school. Visit the "Child Care, Parent Resource" page at www. myflfamilies.com to get tips on:

- Choosing Child Care & Summer Camps

- Know Your Child Care Facility (brochures & checklist)

- Laws - Requirements & Recalls

- Quality Checklist & Family Guide to electing and evaluating Early Learning Programs

When my children were little, I found it was very helpful to attend activities like Family Music Time, Mother's of Preschoolers (MOPS), and Mommy & Me. They gave me great insight on the countless amount of things to do in our area while helping me get to know other moms and parents. Connecting with other parents will make it easy to get truthful referrals and references for everything from your child's doctors to best place to find deals on kids' clothes! Make sure to get a copy of the FREE monthly "Lee Family News" magazine. It is packed with everything you need to know to keep your kids busy. Summer camps, holiday activities, playgroups, and school enrollment information makes raising kids in SWFL a breeze! Check out www. leefamilynews.net for distribution locations. If you are looking for nannies or babysitters in your area, you can go online to www. Nextdoor.com, www.Care.com, and www.SitterCity.com to find the help and support you need.

Voluntary Pre-K Programs

Pre-School Kids Enjoying Books

Across the US our kids are being required to know more when they enter kindergarten. To make sure your child is starting off kindergarten on the right foot, the state of Florida, through the Office of Early Learning, has developed a preschool voucher program that allows your child to attend a Voluntary Pre-Kindergarten class at any of the approved providers in Lee County. If you have found a school and the tuition for that school is greater than the voucher amount, you may still send your child to that school. You would just be responsible to pay the difference between the amount of tuition and the amount of the voucher.

Voluntary PreKindergarten is also referred to as VPK or PK-4. To qualify for the VPK Voucher you will need to visit the Early Learning Coalition of Southwest Florida, either online at www.elcofswfl.org or in person to make sure the child is eligible and fill out an application. The criteria at the time of this printing were pretty simple. You need to be a Florida resident and your child must have turned 4 years old on or before September 1.

Southwest Florida is following other counties around the state with the Quality Rating Improvement System (QRIS). This rating system was implemented by the Early Learning Coalition of Southwest Florida and covers a 4-county area that includes Lee, Collier, Hendry, and Glades County. While they have not publicized results yet, you are encouraged to look for the QRIS Stars when considering a preschool program.

K-12 Education Choices

Choices are the key to success in education. Every child is unique in his or her own way and can benefit greatly from having several options available when it comes to their education. Our county has devoted teachers and administrators who work with parents to ensure that each student achieves his or her highest personal potential.

The Lee County School District is the 33rd largest public-school district in the country and 9th largest district in the State of Florida. Our 120 schools encompass both public and charter schools. For 2018, the school district served over 93,000 students.

Southwest Florida has seen tremendous economic and demographic growth over the years and our county's population growth has soared. This meant our schools previously had to accommodate for rapid annual growth by redrawing school boundaries and uprooting students from their school on an annual basis. That put a great burden on students and their families.

In 1997, the Lee County School District Student Assignment procedure was introduced. Our unified school system has created an abundance of exceptional educational programs that now take Lee County students from classroom to college or directly into careers of their choice, depending on each student's goals.

Check out some of Lee County School Districts Fast Facts as taken from the Lee County School Districts Website:

- 52% of schools receiving an "A" or "B" ranking from the State up from 46% the previous year. Its overall ranking improved from 35th to 30th.

- The District offers 17 different career clusters within our high schools, giving students the opportunity to explore different careers through hands-on learning during their school day.

- The students enrolled in our high school career academies earned thousands of industry certifications each school year, enabling them to graduate high school and enter the workforce with certifications in disciplines such as CompTIA A+, Fire Fighter 1, Certified Nursing Assistant (CNA), Autodesk Certified User (AutoCAD), Dreamweaver, Adobe Flash, Photoshop, and more!

- The District offerings include the prestigious International Baccalaureate (IB) and Cambridge AICE programs at the high school level in each attendance zone.

- The graduates from the School District of Lee County earned $53 million in scholarship monies in 2016.

- Centers for the Arts programs are offered at the elementary, middle, and high school level in each attendance zone. Students take courses in dance, theatre, performing, and visual arts.

- Dunbar High School is the first Microsoft Certified High School in the world. In 2008, Dunbar became the first school in the world to have 100% of its IT Academy students who were enrolled in Microsoft courses successfully achieve certifications.

Visit www.LeeSchools.net "Fast Facts For New Residents" for more information.

Private Schools

Depending on the source and description you can find between 22-50 plus private schools in the Lee County area. They vary greatly in size, cost, and programs offered. There are many faith-based schools including Catholic, Lutheran, Evangelical, and other Christian-World View Schools. Additionally, there is Maimonides Hebrew Day School. There are secular schools as well that include STEM, Montessori, and Dual Enrollment focused curriculum. Private school tuition costs for our area are usually lower than the national average. If cost is a prohibitive factor for you, make sure to inquire if the private school you are interested in has a scholarship or financial aid program. I found two great schools, Canterbury School and Bishop Verot High School, that had these options available to students and families. If you are considering a private school option for your children, you can compare schools at:

www.privateschoolreview.com/florida/lee-county

Understanding the Lee County Public School System

Lee County families have multiple education options to choose from within the Public School System. The Lee County school system assigns students to schools through an open enrollment process.

There are 4 key benefits to the open enrollment process.

- Both parent and child can provide input into choosing and ranking the schools that best fit their needs.

- Proximity zoning means that you are more likely to go to what most people would call a "community" school nearest your home.

- Random lottery creates fairness for all. The lottery allows everyone to have an equal opportunity to attend one of his or her top pick schools.

- Multiple preferences means you can list all the schools in your subzone by rank which gives you multiple opportunities to get a school of your choice.

Once you have made the decision to enroll your child in the Public School System, you will need to proceed with the school selection and ranking process.

The open enrollment process can be simplified into five steps.

1. **Knowing your registration deadlines dates.** Student enrollment registration/application process begins each year in January. The most important date is the enrollment deadline date, it occurs 10 weeks after the 1st application period ends. After this deadline, students will be assigned to schools where the seats are still open. Make sure to visit the www.LeeSchools.net "Understanding Open Enrollment" webpage for the current year's deadlines.

2. **Finding your zone and subzone.** The student assignment plan created 3 large zones that encompass all of Lee County. These zones are the east zone, west zone, and south zones. Within each of these 3 zones, there are 3 subzones. On the map provided on the following page, they are labeled as E-1, E-2, E-3, and W-1, W-2, W-3, and S-1, S-2, S-3. You can view the map to find your zone or you can enter your address into the "Find My School" interactive map and you will be given a list of schools available for that location.

3. **Choosing your schools.** Once you have found your eligible schools based on your home address using the interactive map, you can click the links for each school to find out what each of them have to offer. Each school's website shares the same layout, so you should have an easy time finding information regarding the academic curriculum, electives, school times, and open house dates. You will register your child by ranking all the schools available in your subzone. Make sure to rank all schools. Make

sure to review all school and program requirements, as additional application processes may be required.

4. **Registering your child.** Parents of new Lee County students will need to enroll at the student assignment office located most convenient to them. You will need to bring ALL the required documentation in order to register. A detailed list should be reviewed online at www.LeeSchool.net to ensure you are viewing most up-to-date requirements.

5. **Understanding the process.** The school enrollment process can be confusing for families moving from other types of school systems. If you have questions or concerns you are encouraged to visit the student assignment offices to get more information for your particular situation. www.leeschools.net/student-assignment

THE SCHOOL DISTRICT OF LEE COUNTY

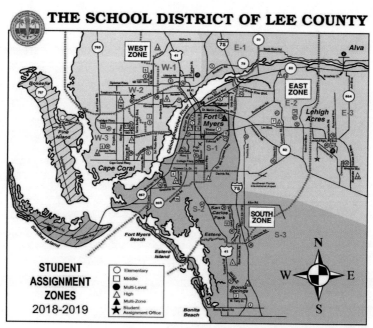

Map of Lee County School District Zones

85

East Zone - Lehigh Acres Office
1262 Wings Way Suite #207, Lehigh Acres, FL 33936
Phone: (239) 337-8347 • Fax: (239) 303-2589

West Zone - Cape Coral Office
360 Santa Barbara Blvd. N., Cape Coral, FL 33993
Phone: (239) 242-2059 • Fax: (239) 458-1079

South Zone - Fort Myers Office
2855 Colonial Blvd., Fort Myers, FL 33966
Phone: (239) 337-8247 • Fax: (239) 335-1428

The School District of Lee County has worked hard to provide diverse and specialized school programs in each of the 3 zones. This creates a neighborhood school system feel with the flexibility of finding the right educational needs for your child. The school district's goal is to have each of the program offerings available within each zone. Here is a list of the program offering and their codes.

- Arts Programs (A)

- Technology Programs (T)

- Science, Technology, Engineering and Math Programs (STEM)

- Comprehensive Programs (C)

- International Baccalaureate Schools (IB)
  Cambridge Programs (CA)

- Foreign Language Program (FL)

- Uniform Required Schools (U)

West Zone Schools	South Zone Schools	East Zone Schools
Elementary Schools	**Elementary Schools**	**Elementary Schools**
Caloosa (U)	Allen Park	The Alva School (K-8)
Cape	Bonita Springs (U) (A)	Bayshore (U)
Diplomat (U)	Colonial (U)	Edgewood Academy (A) (U)
Gulf	Edison Park (A)	G. Weaver Hipps
Hancock Creek	Franklin Park (U)	Gateway
Hector A. Cafferata, Jr. (U)	Heights (IB)	Harns March
J. Colin English (U)(IB)	Orangewood	James Stephens Academy (K-8) (U)
Littleton (U)	Pinewoods	Lehigh
NFM Academy of the Arts (K-8) (A) (U)	Ray V. Pottorf	Manatee (U)
Patriot	Rayma C. Page (U)	Mirror Lakes (U)
Pelican	San Carlos Park (U) (A)	Orange River
Skyline	Spring Creek (U)	River Hall (U)
Trafalgar (U)	Tanglewood	Sunshine
Tropic Isles	Three Oaks	Tice (FL)
	Villas	Tortuga Preserve (U) (STEM)
Middle Schools		Treeline (U)
Caloosa	**Middle Schools**	Veterans Park (K-8) (A) (U)
Challenger	Bonita Springs (A)	
Diplomat	Cypress Lake (A)	**Middle Schools**
Gulf	Fort Myers Middle Academy (U) (T)	The Alva School (K-8)
Mariner (B)	Lexington (IB)	Harns Marsh (U) (STEM)
NFM Academy of the Arts(K-8)(A)(U)	Paul Laurence Dunbar	James Stephens Academy(K-8)(U)
Trafalgar	Three Oaks (U)	Lehigh Acres (U)
		Oak Hammock (U) (A)
High Schools	**High Schools**	Varsity Lakes (U)
Cape Coral (B)	Cypress Lake (A)	Veterans Park (K-8) (A) (U)
Ida S. Baker ©	Dunbar (IB) (STEM)	
Island Coast	Estero (CA)	**High Schools**
Mariner	Fort Myers (IB)	Dunbar (IB) (STEM)
N. Ft. Myers (A) (CA)	South Fort Myers ©	East Lee County ©
		Lehigh Senior (A) (CA)
		Riverdale (IB)

List of Schools by Zone

If you live on one of our barrier islands (Sanibel Island, Pine Island, and Estero Island) your child can attend that island's school as long as your child is within the age level for that school. You do not need to go through the student assignment process unless you wish to apply for your zone or a multi-zone magnet school.

While 95% of students get one of their top choice schools, some do not. You can find more information about waivers, eligibility pools, and re-enrollment along with a complete detailed explanation of the Student Assignment Process online at: www.leeschools.net/student-assignment. The website has several videos, FAQ's, and forms available for download.

Re-enrollment is required when a student moves out of a zone and the zone school is no longer available or when the child has reached the top grade at that school. So, if you are enrolling a kindergartener, like I am this year, you will go through this process a total of 3 times throughout the student's education.

At first, I was like many parents confused by the changes to our school system. Frankly no one likes change. But I also have the benefit of hindsight, since I was also a Lee County student prior to the student assignment system. I see so much more opportunity for middle school and high school students than I did growing up. I am comforted that, as my children grow up in Lee County, they will have the option of taking courses that interest them and will lead them down a career path, whether it be college or straight into the career of choice.

School Registration Quick Tips

- *Gather paperwork to bring to student assignment office.*

- *Use "Find My School" interactive map to get a listing of eligible schools in your subzone.*

- *Research and prioritize schools in your subzone.*

- *Download and complete the student registration form.*

- *Download and complete the student assignment application for your zone & school level.*

- *Download and complete school records release form (if student was enrolled previously in another school).*

- *Bring all completed paperwork and documentation to one of the student assignment offices to register your student. These documents include:*

  - *Photo ID*

  - *Original Birth Certificate*

  - *Social Security Card (if available)*

  - *Health Examination (physical)*

  - *Florida Certificate of Immunization*

  - *Proof of Custody (if child not living with both natural parents)*

  - *Name and address of last school attended)*

  - *Copy of IEP (Individual Education Plan)*

  - *Proof of Address (specific list available online).*

** Some schools and programs may require additional applications. See program and school requirements for more information. Office hours are Monday - Friday 9:00am to 4:00pm. For more information please visit: www.leeschools.net

Career Education

High School Students in Chemistry Class

High School (and some middle schools) can take advantage of Career Education Courses. These courses are designed to help students make informed decisions for their future. Students can learn a variety of skill-sets, including leadership, communication, and other employability skills through hands on training. Completion of these courses can put them ahead of the competition as they seek career opportunities, college or technical school placement.

The following Programs of Study are available:

- Accounting

- Culinary Operations

- Digital Design

- Drafting

- Early Childhood Education

- Networking

- New Media

- Nursing Assistant

- Television Production

- Veterinary Assistant

- Web Development

Visit the Career Academies webpage www.leeschools.net/career-academies to see what Career Clusters are available at which High Schools. Each High School webpage will have more information about that school's Career Academy offerings.

Benefits of School Choice
by Kathy Cole

Many folks feel that the school choice system in Lee County is confusing, particularly when they first relocate to the area. While it can be a bit overwhelming, I have found it to be a system that has really benefited my children. My son, who is a very scientific kid and loves working with his hands rather than listening to a lecture, had the opportunity to choose a high school where he was able to be in both the medical and veterinary academies. By doing so, he really engaged in learning by doing and had the choice to pursue his LPN, phlebotomy or veterinary assistant licensing upon graduation.

Throughout his high school years in these two academies, he was able to narrow his focus to what he really had a passion for and ultimately decided upon getting his veterinary assistant license. He was also recruited through the veterinary program for a job at a local veterinarian's office where he worked after school and remained working there for several years through high school and his early years of college. His opportunities with the academy learning format at South Fort Myers High School provided him hands on experience so that he could not only obtain a job in that field before and after graduation, but also gave him insight as to whether or not he would want to pursue further college education in that field.

My daughter, who is the complete opposite of my son, has always been artsy and creative. Her passion for the arts led her to audition for the Theatre program at Cypress Lake High School where she was admitted and is currently thriving in her sophomore year. The school choice program can be somewhat daunting to a newcomer, but can really be beneficial to children with very different types of needs and interests.

Kathy Cole is the married mother to two Lee County students and is also a Master ISR Instructor serving the Fort Myers area. Infant Swim Rescue instructors teach swimming and self-rescue® skills to children (6 months to 6 years).

Tuition Free Public Charter Schools

Charter schools offer parents tuition-free alternative educational opportunities that are funded by tax dollars. The School Board of Lee County sponsors all public Charter schools. These schools have their own governing body and operate independently. They are held to the same Florida standards and benchmarks as the rest of the districts' schools. Here is a list of some of the larger Charter school providers:

- Charter School USA (www.charterschoolsusa.com)

- Celerity Schools (www.celerityschools.org)

- Cape Charter Schools (www.capecharterschools.org)

These education service providers can partner with the public school system and provide student centered education that is needed within communities. Cape Charter Schools is a great example of this partnership at work. Many of the Charter schools offer a smaller classroom size, flexible morning and/or afternoon course schedules, along with some blended options like the ones offered at Pivot Charter School that allow you to attend school online. Below is a list of Lee County Approved Charter Schools. This list can also be found on the www.LeeSchools.net website.

- Acceleration Middle School

- Athenian Academy Charter School

- Bonita Springs Charter School

- Cape Coral Charter School

- Christa McAuliffe Charter Elementary School

- City of Palms Charter High School

- Coronado High School

- Donna J. Beasley Technical Academy

- Florida Southwestern Collegiate High School - Lee

- Gateway Charter Elementary School

- Gateway Charter Intermediate School

- Gateway Charter High School

- Harlem Heights Community Charter School

- Island Park High School

- The Island School

- North Nicholas High School

- Northern Palms Charter High School

- Oak Creek Charter School of Bonita Springs

- Oasis Charter Elementary School

- Oasis Charter Middle School

- Oasis Charter High School

- Palm Acres Charter High School

- Six Mile Charter Academy

- Unity Charter School of Cape Coral

- Unity Charter School of Fort Myers

Parents choose Charter Schools for a variety of reasons: academics, electives, classroom sizes, and flexible course schedules are all attractive benefits that families can appreciate.

Adult Education - Non-Degree Programs and Special Centers

Adult and Career Education Programs, also referred to as ACE, are programs offered by the Lee County School District to students and adults. They are broken down into two main categories. Visit the www.leeschools.net/ace website for more information.

- Adult Education can help students reach their potential. Whether it is re-taking the Florida Comprehensive Assessment Test (FCAT), earning their High School Diploma through the GED Prep & Testing courses, learning English as a Second Language (ESOL) or taking one of the many Life Long Learning Classes. Lee County Schools encourages all to continue their education and invest in your future.

- Special Centers - Lee County School District fulfills the needs of the community by offering Education Centers with Special Programs. The following are some of the Special Centers offered: Cape Coral Technical College, Dunbar Community School, Fort Myers Technical College, Southwest Florida Public Service Academy, Alternative Learning Centers (ALC), Lee Virtual Instruction Program, and PACE Center for Girls.

Lee County students have so many options it can be a bit overwhelming for parents. I encourage you to visit some of the links below that can help you find out more about our schools.

- Lee County School District Main Website
  www.leeschools.net

- Lee County School Foundation
  www.leeschoolfoundation.org

- Facebook - www.facebook.com/schooldistrictofleecounty

- Twitter - www.twitter.com/leeschools (#LoveLeeSchools)

- You Tube - www.youtube.com/user/LeeSchools

The District works hard to keep information flowing to students and to parents. These social media sites have tons of great information to keep you in the loop. If you have further questions, please contact the school board or the schools directly.

Homeschooling

Our county has also been a strong supporter of homeschooling. This support shines brightly through the www.LeeVirtualSchool. com website. The school board chose the easy to follow Calvert's Curriculum to work side by side with parents who wish to homeschool their children. This partnership helps ensure that your child meets national and state standards.

If you choose to homeschool in Florida, you need to establish a Home Education Program. This may sound difficult, but based on my research with several homeschooling groups, it is very easy to homeschool in Lee County. The www.LeeSchools.net website has everything you need to get started. The "essential documents" include:

- Home Education Packet - PDF

- Notice of Intent to Establish Home Education Program - Form

- Annual Evaluation Notice - Form

The school district has an extra-curricular interscholastic activities program that may be an option for your child. It appears that if a child is enrolled in the virtual schools they are more likely to be eligible, versus if a child is enrolled in a Non-Traditional Private School also known as an "Umbrella School" or a "600 School". These students are not eligible to take part in the extracurricular activities program. Visit the school board's website for more information on how your child may qualify before choosing your Home Education Program.

In the event you wish to transfer out of the Home Education Program, you will also need to complete the Notice of Termination of Home Education Program Form. If you have more questions or want to get started, visit:

The Lee County Public Education Center
Department of Student Welfare and Attendance
Daily between 8:00am and 4:30pm, 337-8259
2855 Colonial Boulevard
Ft. Myers, FL 33966-1012

Homeschooling laws can change on a national, state, and even local level. Finding and then joining a local homeschool co-op group can keep you in the loop locally and following sites like Homeschool Legal Defense Association (www.hslda.org) online, can keep you informed on a national level. Here is a list of homeschool resources that you should find helpful:

- Lee Virtual School www.leevirtualschool.com (K-5 Virtual Public Homeschool)

- Florida Virtual School www.flvs.net (K-12 Virtual Public Homeschool)

- Classical Christian Academy www.discovercca.com (Hybrid)

- Grace Classical Academy www.graceclassicalflorida.com (Hybrid)

- Heart And Home Homeschoolers www.heartnhome.org (Co-op)

- Classical Conversations www.classicalconversations.com (Co-op)

- SWFL Homeschooling Families (Co-op)

- Gulf Coast Homeschool Association (Co-op)

- Lehigh Acres Homeschool Groups (Co-op)

The co-op groups are facilitated by the parents, so keep in mind the website pages can change. I listed the names of some of the long-standing clubs that should be easy to find by going online and searching for their names. Also listed are 2 of the hybrid homeschool options. These are popular options for parents that would like to have a more structured learning environment. These schools have 3 or 4-day in-school classroom options along with sports, electives, and various school events and competitions held throughout the year.

College & University Choices

The Academic Core at FGCU

Florida Gulf Coast University

10501 FGCU Blvd South, Fort Myers, FL 33965
(239) 590-1000 www.fgcu.edu

Florida Gulf Coast University (FGCU) enrolls 14,480 students a year and is located off Ben Hill Griffin Parkway east of I-75 between Alico Road and Corkscrew Road exits. It is a medium size regional 4-year public university that offers associate, bachelors, masters, and doctorate degrees. Popular majors include business, marketing, management, communication, journalism, education, health professional, and psychology. It is accredited through the Southern Association of Colleges and Schools. FGCU is also a stand out in their athletic department, too. They became nationally known in 2013 when this hometown division 1 men's basketball team went on to the NCAA Sweet 16 regional semifinals. This stunning achievement for the whole school put FGCU "Dunk City" on the map! On campus housing can accommodate 4750 students with additional off campus housing available nearby. On campus housing makes the 2018 top 10 list of "Best College Dorms in America" as reported by Niche.com

Florida Southwestern State College

8099 College Parkway, Fort Myers, Florida, 33919
(239) 489-9300 www.fsw.edu

Florida Southwestern State College (FSW) has their main campus right in the heart of Fort Myers at the intersection of College Parkway and Summerlin Road. Originally a small junior college known as Edison Community College, it has grown to include 4 campuses in Lee, Collier, Charlotte, and Hendry/Glades Counties that serve 16,830 students. Associates and bachelor's degrees in the fields of arts, humanities, sciences, business, technology, education, and health professionals are available at this college.

Ave Maria University

5050 Ave. Maria Boulevard, Ave Maria, FL 34142
(239) 280-2500 www.avemaria.edu

Ava Maria University (AMU) is located further south in the town of Ava Maria, Florida, which is located southeast of Lee County. It is a private national liberal arts Catholic University that serves 1100 students. They offer 29 different majors including accounting, biochemistry, economics, finance, a theology graduate program, and a study abroad program.

Other Colleges & Universities

Several other local colleges offer career focused education options in a variety of fields like criminal justice, education, law, information technology, networking, health care, nursing, drafting/design, digital media, and communication. Here is a list of colleges with local campuses. Most offer online classes, too. Please see each college for specific course offerings.

- Ave Maria School of Law - www.avemarialaw.edu

- Barry University - www.barry.edu

- Hodges University - www.hodges.edu

- ITT-Technical Institute - www.itt-tech.edu

- Keiser University - www.keiser-education.com

- Nova Southeastern University - www.nova.edu

- Rasmussen College - www.rasmussen.edu

- Southern Technical College - www.southerntech.edu

Almost every college that I researched offered some type of scholarship and student loan program. A great place to start is the Florida Department of Education, Office of Student Financial Assistance webpage (www.floridastudentfinancialaid.org). You will find information for student loans, grants, scholarships, and applications. It also has a link to the Florida Automated System for Transferring Educational Records (FASTER) and the Florida Department of Education website (www.fldoe.org).

CHAPTER 8

CHOOSING THE RIGHT COMMUNITY: A COMPREHENSIVE GUIDE

The types of housing communities in Southwest Florida are as diverse as our residents' hobbies and interests. It's important to keep in mind where you plan to spend your time while choosing a corner of the county to call home. In this section, I'll guide you through the North, East, West, and South areas of the county to find out what type of homes your will find:

- Who are your neighbors?

- What can your money buy?

- Which schools are in this sections proximity zone preference?

Having this understanding of the unique corners of our county will help you and your real estate professional find the perfect home in paradise for you!

North County

Greater Fort Myers is a magnet for an eclectic group of people from all walks of life. We attract boaters, beachcombers, young families, sports enthusiasts, golfers, retirees, and snowbirds (just to name a few) that flock to Greater Fort Myers to call it home. A rich variety of different types of communities welcome you. To narrow your search, we need to determine your budget.

Budget

When it comes to budgets and financing a home in Greater Fort Myers, you need to consider the unique costs of living here. That includes the extra costs of gated communities and the possible need for flood insurance.

Gated communities typically have HOA (Home Owner Association) Fees. The benefit of an HOA is they do so much to maintain the beauty of the neighborhood and the upkeep on common areas that may include clubhouses, pools, golf courses, tennis courts, basketballs courts. And some of the larger communities include town centers. Since potential neighborhoods give you so many amenities, you must take this into account when you explore desirable neighborhoods.

Another expense to keep in mind is flood insurance. You can consult the FEMA (Federal Emergency Management Agency) maps here: www.leegov.com/gis/maps/printable-maps/firm. It will help you identify which areas are in a zone that requires flood insurance (Zone X does not require flood insurance at this time). Even if you are not required to carry flood insurance, you may still want to obtain a policy. Your local mortgage lender can help you run the numbers, get prequalified, pre-approved, and give you referrals of insurance agencies to call for quotes. Using local lenders, insurance agents, and realtors helps to ensure accurate estimates of fees along with a timely closing.

Home Features

The next critical step is to create a need/want list. Make a list of what you and your family absolutely *"have to have"* items and then add to that list the things that you wish to have. Discuss this list with your realtor so she has a clear understanding of what to look for. Many older homes with a little work could become your dream home.

You can also use popular websites like Trulia and Zillow to look at home styles and community amenities. They are great for getting to know the area. But, beware the information on these homes are sometimes owner generated listings that are not real-time. So, what you see may be inaccurate. That's one more reason why a local licensed real estate agent is imperative.

Location, Location, Location

That perennial real estate phrase still rings true and reinforces the vital importance of your location. How close are the best schools? How long a commute to our jobs? How close to shopping?

The 2 most popular questions for the diehard boater, fisherman, and beachcomber:

- How long a drive to the beach?
- How long is the boat ride to the Gulf?

Communities like Miromar Lakes have created massive beautiful inland boating lakes right within the confines of their community. So, the best thing to ask yourself, is what is important to you?

* Love boating, nature, wildlife, beach coming? Check out Northern and Western Lee County.

* Love shopping, restaurants, nightlife? Check out the City of Fort Myers, Eastern, and Southern Lee County.

* Love spending time with your family? Then find a home near your work, so you cut down on commute time.

You can also learn a lot by just visiting the local grocery store and people watching. You will see if it is mostly retirees, families or tourists wearing swimsuit coverups. Consider staying at an Air BnB during your visit versus a hotel. This will give you an insight to how it would actually be living in your potential "new town".

Finding a Realtor

It may seem that we have just as many realtors as homes for sale. What some might think is a problem is really a benefit to buyers because you can usually find a realtor that specializes in your ideal home or community. I have seen specialists for everything from equestrian homes to aeronautical homes with landing strips.

A quick search online will help you locate three realtors to call. Then use this quick questionnaire to help identify the right realtor for you:

- Do you work with a team or have an assistant?

- How long do your typical buyers take to find a home and close?

- In which communities do you do the most business?

- What is your procedure for showings?

- What is the best way to communicate and collaborate on our search for a home?

Annual and Seasonal Renting Options

If you haven't had a chance to experience our area in person before your move, then renting can be a great way to test the waters of communities before you buy. Renting for a year or even just a season can give you the experience of living like a local. You can check out neighborhood restaurants, cafe's, grocery stores, and talk to the locals to ask their opinion of nearby communities.

Depending on your budget, the rental market can be very tight and quick moving. If renting is something you are considering, start the search right away as it may take longer than normal to find home available for annual rentals.

Our area has a lot of snowbirds and visitors, so this also means we have a lot of seasonal rentals. Make sure to double check your rental agreement to make sure it is for an annual basis without penalty or extra fees.

Buying in the Greater Fort Myers Area
by Chris Black

Over the last 10 years of working in real estate in Southwest Florida, I've heard the following a lot of times: "Well, in [insert a snowbird state], we don't do it like that." We understand. Things are different here in Florida and because of that the real estate experience can often be confusing and overwhelming. In addition to the items below, the best piece of advice I can give you is to keep an open mind and to trust in the professionals with whom you have chosen to work.

Do I Need an Attorney?

In many states, attorney participation in real estate transactions is required. This is especially true in the Mid-Atlantic, in New England and in the Carolinas. In Florida, having an attorney involved in your transaction is not required. A state licensed title insurance agency may handle just about every facet of your transaction – from holding and disbursing funds to drafting documents to issuing title insurance – to provide peace of mind and to protect your property rights.

One thing to note here is that a title insurance agency cannot represent your individual interests as an attorney could. They are limited to performing acts related to the issuance of title insurance. Should you want the independent representation of an attorney, I would encourage you to hire one.

Who Pays for What?

Florida is not unlike most other jurisdictions in that the obligation to pay for closing costs is a contractual issue. You are more than welcome to negotiate which party pays for which fees. That said, there are certain customs related to closing costs which you may encounter when buying and selling in Florida. In most counties (except for Collier), the seller customarily pays for the buyer's owner's policy of title insurance. Our standard form residential real estate contracts place the burden of paying for the documentary stamp taxes on the deed on the seller. And, buyers should expect to pay for all costs related to their home loan (e.g., lender fees, lender's title insurance, mortgage recording fees, etc.).

Do I Have to Be Here for Closing?

We get this question quite a lot and I am happy to report that you do not have to be here to complete your closing. While we would love to see your smiling faces and personally hand you the keys to your new piece of paradise, it is not at all necessary. Your closing documents can be sent overnight or even by email; and, your funds will be sent or delivered by wire transfer.

If you have questions about buying a home in our area, please don't hesitate to call.

Chris Black Attorney & Owner of Winged Foot Title, LLC
8695 College Parkway, Suite 2350
Fort Myers, Florida 33919
P: (239) 985-4142 / W: www.wingedfoottitle.com
Blog: www.homeclosingprocess.com

My goal with this book is to teach you all the reasons you will love your new home and community. As a critical part of that effort, the following sections preview the 4 corners of our county.

First, let's start where it all began, the City of Fort Myers.

The City of Fort Myers most desired neighborhoods are located along the McGregor Corridor. Unlike many of the upscale residential communities in SWFL, the McGregor district does not have gates. If you are looking for a neighborhood with sidewalks where neighbors stroll for a sunset walk to the river's edge—or bike or jog along the palm lined McGregor Boulevard, then start your home search here.

It has the most northern feel with lots of beautiful older homes and mature landscaping. The west (river) side of McGregor Blvd. has million-dollar mansions that sit on the Caloosahatchee River. You will also find many historic homes in the area that were built around the turn of the century. As you move further south down McGregor and on the East side of the boulevard, you will find more mid-century construction homes. Many have been remodeled and updated to optimize their unique designs.

Who are your neighbors?

Aerial View of Downtown Fort Myers

106

The downtown area has beautiful high-rises and low-rise condominiums such as High Point Place, Beau Rivage, and the upcoming Prima Luce that offer breathtaking views of the river and offer a variety of amenities that cater to the people who work downtown. And many are millennials. Retirees also enjoy the maintenance free living and the wealth of entertainment and dining options just steps away.

What can your money buy?

The most reliable real time real estate data is found in the Royal Palm Coast Realtor Association or www.swflrealtors.com. The Realtors Multiple Listing Service has a unique geographic coding system referred to as Geo Codes.

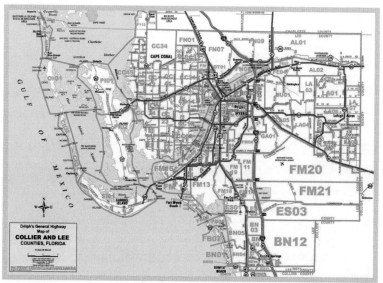

Geo Code Map

To give you an idea of the current homes for sale in the 3 most desirable geographic areas (GEO Codes DT01, FM01, FM02), here is a range of prices for different types of homes you can find in this area:

Downtown Riverfront High rise condos sell from the upper $200,000s to well over $1 million and $200,000 can get you a very nice older low-rise condo.

McGregor Boulevard Single Family Homes can hit $1,795,000 or more for waterfront mansions. But prices are much more affordable as you move east towards the commercial area of US 41. You can find remodeled homes from the $300,000 to $500,000 range and fixer-uppers can be found in the $200,000 range.

Annual rental prices range from $1500 to $2000, whereas seasonal rentals range from $3000 to $4500 a month.

Beautiful Beau Rivage Condo in Downtown Fort Myers
Courtesy: Stacey Glenn of TeamStacey.com

High-rise Living Downtown
by Robert MacFarlane

We asked Bob MacFarlane, a major contributor to the renaissance of downtown Fort Myers and to wonderful high-rise living options, to share his personal and professional thoughts. Here's his insightful overview:

Hello, I'm Bob MacFarlane, CEO of The MacFarlane Barney Group and a proud resident of Fort Myers since 2001.

For me, Fort Myers is a jewel in the crown of Southwest Florida, with all the facets of a great city, especially its beautiful, historic downtown on the banks of the Caloosahatchee River.

Downtown Fort Myers is a diverse community that combines Florida's breathtaking natural beauty and small-town charm with the excitement of a big city steeped in arts and culture, and I strive to develop structures that reflect this unique area and the people that live, work and play here – people like me.

Over the past 17 years as both a developer and a citizen, my dedication and passion for revitalizing Downtown Fort Myers has manifested in four waterfront tower condominium communities. The Beau Rivage opened in October of 2004, followed soon after by Riviera and St. Tropez, and these three buildings were the first waterfront towers after a decades-long pause in development of the Historic River District.

Campo Felice Independent Living

My latest completed project, the fourth tower, which was spearheaded by my daughter Rebekah MacFarlane Barney, is Campo Felice Independent Living, a $90 million renovation and total transformation of the formerly vacant Sheraton Harbor Hotel into a luxury rental community for independent seniors age 55 and up.

Helping people live better lives has and will always be my goal and driving inspiration. I grew up in poverty and I think, perhaps, because I had so little, I grew to greatly appreciate the value of things. I also learned that quality doesn't have to and shouldn't be sacrificed for the sake of a cheaper price tag.

The communities I develop offer both value and quality for a wide range of people from a wide range of income levels, because ultimately, it's the people who bring these communities to life. For me, community development means more people living better lives in Downtown Fort Myers, which will strengthen the area and fuel the steady growth of this great little city.

I recently won a bid to develop a modern, high-quality affordable housing community near downtown, and my current project, also managed by my daughter, is the luxury waterfront condominium community Prima Luce, located on First Street east of the Edison bridge.

Prima Luce consists of two high-rise towers featuring resort-style amenities, including a three-tiered swimming pool, state-of-the-art fitness center, and 325 feet of direct river frontage. A variety of floor plans are available, and each of the 220 residences, which range from $220,000 to $1 million, feature stunning waterfront views.

Prima Luce will be home to the fifth and sixth tower we have been fortunate enough to build in Downtown Fort Myers, and it's going to be the first high-rise development to emerge downtown since the recession – but it won't be the last.

Throughout the course of my nearly 50 years in residential and commercial real estate, I've helped developed communities in Florida, New York, Texas and Connecticut.

Fort Myers will always be home.

How are the schools?

Choosing a home in this area puts you in a prime spot for getting into a great school. Edison Park Creative & Expressive Arts School, Allen Park Elementary, Tanglewood Elementary along with several parochial schools are in this area. All are top rated schools with great reviews. The 100+ year old Fort Myers High School is an award winning International Baccalaureate school that also excels in a variety of sports programs.

Let's move on to the other corners of Lee County to uncover the neighbors, the communities, and the cost to live there!

Northern Lee County

The northern section of Lee County hugs the north side of the Caloosahatchee and includes North Fort Myers and the Bayshore "Country Corridor" east of Interstate 75 all the way out to Alva and Babcock Ranch off of US Highway 31. Country living is the best way to summarize this area. If you need acreage and freedom from HOA's, then this is a great place to start your search.

You can also choose to go "off the electric grid" by moving to the first solar powered city in the United States, Babcock Ranch. This 17,000-acre community also includes 91,000 acres of preserved land. Babcock Ranch is one of the most exciting communities to watch grow since Thomas Edison first built Seminole Lodge.

The homes in this area are typically not gated communities and cater to those that love nature and animals. Large oak hammocks that are dripping with Spanish moss create picturesque scenes for homeowners. Oxbows and creeks create a haven for bird and wildlife viewing along with spectacular sunsets and sunrises. You will find animal and nature lovers at every turn whether it be an equestrian ranch, citrus fields, and even an alpaca farm nestled along the banks of Telegraph Creek.

Who are your neighbors?

You'll find people who appreciate a slower pace, peace and quiet, and stargazing under a dark night's sky. They are business owners, entrepreneurs, retirees with a need for space to enjoy their hobbies, and an occasional Florida Cracker. You will also find boaters and fisherman that enjoy the river life over the salty Gulf of Mexico.

What can your money buy?

- North Fort Myers, Alva, and Buckingham primarily comprise single family homes on spacious and premium lots. Recently, there were 68 homes for sale starting at 2500 square feet. The GEO Codes are AL01 AL02 BU01 FN01 FN02 FN03 FN04 FN07 FN08 FN09 FN10. These homes have a range of features like large acreage, golf course frontage, horse stables, riverfront, and even mansions with airplane hangars and runways for your personal aircraft. Prices range from $337,000 up to $3,800,000.

- **Burnt Store Marin**a recently had 59 homes for sale ranging from $92,000 for a small villa to $795,000 for a 4000 square foot 2 story marina front condo.

- **Babcock Ranc**h begins in the upper $300,000s for single family to over $1 million. And new builders are working on options for villas that will start in the $200,000 range.

Due to the unique nature of the homes in this area few rentals are typically available.

How are the schools?

The top-rated schools from Greatschools.org for this area are Bayshore Elementary, Tropic Isles Elementary, North Fort Myers For the Arts, and North Fort Myers High School. But, if you are considering moving to the area and have school aged kids, visit the Babcock Neighborhood School. This school sits in the Charlotte County district but is a charter school that also takes Lee County students through a second-tier lottery application process. Since this community and school is new it's easier to find a place for your children. This is a GreenSTEAM approach school which includes art and environmental education.

Eastern Lee County

Eastern Lee County continues with that country feel for much of Lehigh Acres. This community covers 95 square miles and started to develop around the 1950's. Like Cape Coral, Lehigh Acres has had real estate booms and busts over the years. But it still has the big draw of being affordable, which makes it easier to find a starter home.

As you make your way to the Colonial Boulevard and Treeline Avenue area, you will see more manicured lawns with gated entrances. One of the most notable communities is Gateway, which gets its namesake from the 30 gated communities within the Gateway (Taxing) District. When considering your budget, you will need to look closely at the tax bill as some of the normal HOA fees you would expect may instead show up in your annual tax bill. Follow www.GatewaySun.com for more information about Gateway.

Who are your neighbors?

Lehigh Acres price point makes it affordable for new families starting out. Gateway also is home to one of the largest employers, Gartner Group, so you will find many of their employees in the area. The Fort Myers City Limits area also attracts a lot of commuter families and retirees that love to golf and travel. Easy access to I75 and RSW International Airport makes this the perfect area for the north-south hop from work to home.

What can your money buy?

- **Lehigh Acres** covers a large section of Lee County and had 3400 homes listed for sale at this writing. Since it's farthest from the beaches, it also has more affordable options. The median home price in Lehigh Acres is $159,500. This would buy you a 1500 square foot home without a pool. Stick to streets with newer homes with few rentals (better curb appeal compared to older homes or rentals).

- **Gateway Communities** had 129 homes, villas, and/or condos for sale starting at $116,000 ranging to $849,000. You'll find many wonderful options in this community.

- **Fort Myers City Limits** covers GEO area FM20 FM21 FM22 had over 433 homes and/or condos available starting as low at $109,900 on up to mansions in Miromar Lakes Beach & Golf Club for $4,895,000. The Treeline/Ben Hill Griffith Parkway corridor has a number of well-established and desirable subdivisions like Colonial Country Club, Pelican Preserve, and Botanica Lakes.

Rentals run from $1000 to $3000 for a single-family home of 1200 to 3000 square feet. The gated communities sometimes include basic cable, internet, and lawn care in the monthly rent.

How are the schools?

Public Schools with the highest Greatschools.org rating in this area are Veterans Park Academy for the Arts, Varsity Lakes Middle School, Sunshine Elementary School, and Gateway Charter Schools.

Southern Lee County

This is the corner I call home. South Fort Myers covers a large area, but we will concentrate on the Summerlin Road, Daniels Parkway area along with a brief introduction to the Estero and Bonita area. If you want to be close to beaches, entertainment, great schools, parks, shopping, and restaurants, this is the place! Like most of the county, you will find a variety of different subdivisions. Some gated, some not.

Who are your neighbors?

You'll find a mixture of snowbirds, professionals with families, and younger people entering the workforce. They all want quick access to the island beaches, the arts and entertainment of downtown Fort Myers, and the shopping of Gulf Coast Town Center, Miromar Outlet Mall, and Coconut Point. I personally love being 15-25 minutes away from all three places.

> We have a pretty good neighborhood village, or at least I think we do. We do driveway nights almost every Friday where the kids play and ride bikes while the adults get to relax in lawn chairs. If I need an egg or a bottle of wine, I make a call to a neighbor who usually comes right over with it. My husband and I know every person on our street by name and we have their phone numbers too. We were raised this way and we feel our children should be raised the same.
>
> *Jenny Baleat, Resident of Whiskey Creek*

What can your money buy?

Lakefront Coach Homes

South Fort Myers has a vast number of unique gated communities and meandering neighborhoods of varying ages, amenities, and styles. From Geo Code area FM05 through FM19 there were 1687 homes available.

- Older South Fort Myers had 1200 square feet homes without pools starting at $150,000 in San Carlos Park. Fort Myers Villas start at around $190,000 and $250,000 in Whiskey Creek for a similar type of home.

- Newer South Fort Myers communities start at $259,000 for a 1776 square foot home in Paseo, Coast Key, Mirada, Banyan Bay, Daniels Place, Coconut Cove, Camden Square, Cypress Walk, Heritage Farms, and several of the communities off of Winker Road Extension.

- Luxury Estate Communities These communities with base home prices starting at $600,000 include Gulf Harbour, Devonwood, Briarcliff, Pinecrest, Catalpa Cove, Shenandoah, Hidden Harbor, St Charles Harbour, Jonathan Harbour, Belle Meade, Town and River.

- Sanibel, Captiva and Fort Myers Beach had 655 units on the market as of this writing. Prices are typically less for a Fort Myers Beach property (since there is more inventory available) than a Sanibel property. And Captiva home prices can be even higher. The more peace and quiet you get the higher the price tag. For $22,095,000 you can own "The Mandalay," a Mediterranean inspired villa on the beach that connects Sanibel and Captiva.

- Estero had 1143 listings on the market with a median price of $325,000 at $177/square foot. You can find a wide range of choices from small condos to luxury mansions in Estero.

- Bonita Springs had 1770 listings with a median price of $395,000 at $209/square foot. Like Estero you have an excellent selection of home choices from very affordable to very expensive.

There were 129 annual rentals starting as low as $800 for a one bedroom off Summerlin Road, but you will find more in the $2500 to $3000 range for around a 2200 square foot home.

How are the schools?

Heights Elementary, Three Oaks Elementary, Rayma C. Page Elementary are all top-rated schools in this area. Cypress Middle and High School shine academically as well as artistically. If you have a son or daughter who excels in sports, Lexington Middle School and South Fort Myers High School have excellent sports programs. South Fort Myers High also has a veterinary program. Estero High is a Cambridge International School and also a licensed Medical Academy.

Western Lee County

Beautiful Canal Front Home

The largest city area wise is Cape Coral and takes up a majority of the western part of Lee County. But we can't forget the barrier islands; Sanibel, Captiva, Pine Island, and Fort Myers Beach (Estero Island) are great places to live also.

Who are your neighbors?

People just like me! I originally moved to Cape Coral in 1985, attended Gulf Middle and Cape Coral High School. My first job was at an ice cream joint right down the street from my house. Cape Coral used to be a place you lived, but to buy anything you would have to drive over to Fort Myers. But it has changed so much in the 21st century. It's recent popularity has pushed the population over the 150,000 mark back in 2010 and to 186,970 in 2018. The Cape now attracts great businesses, restaurants, and festivals. Even though I now live in Fort Myers, I still make it a point to head to Cape Coral, where I can enjoy my favorite restaurants and stores.

What can your money buy?

- More than 3400 Cape Coral homes were for sale starting at $109,000 all the way up to $5,900,000. The median listing price was $266,500 in 2018. You can find pretty much any type of home you can imagine here. You'll find lots of affordable and desirable choices. For example, in the $300,000 to $500,000 range you can buy either a newer home off water with a pool or an older home on the water.

- REAL ESTATE TIPS: If you want sailboat access with no bridge access to the gulf, you need to buy a home that is on the south or east side of Del Prado Boulevard and Cape Coral Parkway or on the west side of Burnt Store Road. Use a realtor that specializes in Cape Coral waterfront to get a better understanding of bridges, canal depth, and canal construction. Much of the inner Cape Coral waterfront lots are freshwater canals, so they might give you a nice peaceful and private green-space to view, it will not get you to the Gulf!

How are the schools?

The City of Cape Coral Charter School Authority is a group under the Lee County School District that operates the Cape Coral Charter schools. The public schools also carry a good rating, but the schools that thrive are the ones with really active PTA's, and that is where the Charter School shines.

CHAPTER 9

THE ECONOMY

From the beginning Fort Myers has attracted the most brilliant minds from Edison, Ford, Firestone. And the fire or shall we say "lightbulb" still burns bright here.

Casual Business Meeting

Our beautiful weather not only attracts visitors to vacation here, but also our welcoming economic climate delivers the perfect environment for business owners to grow their companies.

The Cape Coral-Fort Myers metro area tops Forbes' 2017 list of America's fastest growing cities. Anticipated growth: population,

119

3.6%; employment, 3.8%; output 6.8% (thanks to expanding hospitality and housing markets).

Why do we continue to grow? Business Florida wrote that the "Exceptional quality of life, affordable site prices, dynamic work forces make SWFL a big attractor to industries such as healthcare, business services, logistics, and manufacturing"

"Executives see SWFL as not just a place to vacation, but a place to live like you are on vacation while you continue to work in the businesses that you love."

Sources of Greater Fort Myers Economic Strength

- Significant population growth

- Economic expansion, real GDP in Florida continues to grow

- Strong employment growth versus the US and Florida as a whole

- The need for a skilled and well-educated workforce

- A business-friendly climate

- Being a terrific place to live

- Affordable housing

Whether your goal is to build a bustling business, relocate your corporate headquarters or to find a meaningful career, Lee County has the resources to make your dreams a reality.

Florida: A Very Good Place to Do Business

In recent months, banks, private equity and hedge fund firms are finding favorable business conditions in Florida. According to the Tax Foundation, Florida is the fourth-most-favorable state in the nation to do business, behind Alaska, South Dakota, and Wyoming. By comparison, California, New York, and New Jersey are at the bottom as the least favorable states. The recent moves by some businesses to

Florida show the interest in taking advantage of the lack of a state income tax.

Efforts to diversify are taking root. Today, some of the top companies in our area, as reported by Business Observer, are now healthcare-related operations and tech firms.

Greater Fort Myers: A Terrific Place to Do Business

Our metro area boasted a 3.3% unemployment rate vs. the Florida rate of 3.6%, and the U.S. rate of 4.1% in October 2017, according to the Bureau of Labor Statistics.

As indicated by the Southwest Florida Economic Development Alliance:

Recently, Forbes highlighted the Cape Coral-Fort Myers metro area as the best city for future job growth. The Lee County region is expected to add jobs at a 3.9% annual rate compared to the 1.4% national average, a promising figure for southwest Florida.

There's a reason that Fortune 500 companies like Hertz chose to nestle their headquarters in southwest Florida. Florida has continuously ranked #1 for business climate. Paired with a decreasing unemployment rate and increasing job growth rate, there's more incentive than ever. The beaches certainly help as well.

Projected Population Growth of Southwest Florida Lee County Leads the Way

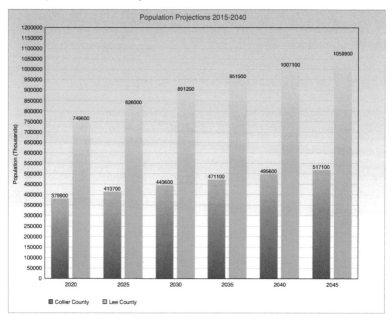

Low Unemployment-Now and Into the Future

According to the Lutgert School of Business at FGCU, the September 2017 economic forecast projects continued declines in unemployment through 2019, with an average forecast close to 4.0 percent for the rest of 2017, 2018, and 2019, and then rising in the long run.

The lower range forecast now falls below 4 percent in 2018 and remains there for two years. If the U.S. economy avoids falling into a recession past the summer of 2019—an outcome consistent with the Fed's projections—then the current expansion will be the longest one observed in 150 years.

Employment by Industry
Lots of Diversity in Types of Employers

Industry	Feb-18	Feb-17	Change
Total Nonagricultural Employment	268,800	267,500	1,300
Total Private	225,100	223,900	1,200
Goods Producing	32,600	32,900	-300
Mining, Logging, and Construction	26,700	27,000	-300
Manufacturing	5,900	5,900	0
Service Providing	236,200	234,600	1,600
Private Service Providing	192,500	191,000	1,500
Trade, Transportation, and Utilities	55,500	54,500	1,000
Wholesale Trade	7,400	7,600	-200
Retail Trade	43,200	42,000	1,200
Food and Beverage Stores	9,100	8,600	500
General Merchandise Stores	6,900	7,200	-300
Transportation, Warehousing, and Utilities	4,900	4,900	0
Information	2,800	2,900	-100
Financial Activities	13,800	13,400	400
Professional and Business Services	37,400	34,700	2,700
Education and Health Services	29,900	29,400	500
Leisure and Hospitality	41,600	44,300	-2,700
Other Services	11,500	11,800	-300

Source: Florida Department of Economic Opportunity

Annual Compensation: Top 25 Occupations

Occupation	Annual Mean Wage
Surgeons	$278,450
Internists, General	$274,940
Pediatricians, General	$252,540
Family and General Practitioners	$244,390
Anesthesiologists	$220,820
Nurse Anesthetists	$203,020
Physicians and Surgeons, All Other	$201,820
Chief Executives	$196,410
Podiatrists	$196,060
Dentists, General	$135,740
Sales Managers	$133,930
Medical and Health Services Managers	$129,590
Personal Financial Advisors	$126,970
Financial Managers	$124,440
Computer and Information Systems Managers	$122,650
General and Operations Managers	$121,620
Pharmacists	$120,080
Architectural and Engineering Managers	$117,630
Sales Representatives, Wholesale and Manufacturing, Technical and Scientific Products	$111,940
Lawyers	$109,980
Purchasing Managers	$109,830
Management Occupations	$105,030
Industrial Production Managers	$104,520
Physician Assistants	$104,050
Education Administrators, Elementary and Secondary School	$102,030

Source: Bureau of Labor Statistics

Major Employers In Southwest Florida

Let's take a look at the some of the major employers that call Southwest Florida home.

Larger corporations are choosing to relocate their corporate headquarters or place a company branch in Lee County and Southwest Florida.

- Arthrex, a privately-held medical device company that develops new products in the field of orthopedics, is headquartered out of Naples. Its workforce of nearly 3,000 is housed within several buildings off Creekside Boulevard. It also has offices in Ave Maria and continues to expand its facilities in Naples.

- NeoGenomics Laboratories, a publicly traded company specializing in genetic testing for cancer, is headquartered in Fort Myers. It employs approximately 130 people locally. In 2015, it acquired Clarient, another well-known and well-regarded national cancer diagnostics laboratory. And in 2016, it built a bigger and better lab to integrate the two.

- Gartner Inc., an information technology research and advisory company, has a branch in Fort Myers where it employs well over 1,000. It continues to grow and has expectations to hire another 900 people by 2019.

- Chico's FAS dates back to 1983 as a small boutique store on Sanibel Island. Today, headquartered in Fort Myers, it encompasses Chico's, White House Black Marketa, and Soma Intimates boutiques and outlets.

- Heinz North America has a manufacturing branch in Fort Myers that produces some of the company's frozen specialties and frozen pastries.

- Hertz Corporation moved its world headquarters from New Jersey to a 34-acre parcel in Estero where a 300,000-square-foot facility with car rental and sales operations houses at least 700 employees.

- Structure Medical, headquartered in Naples, manufactures medical implant products used by orthopedic surgeons. Since opening in 2004, it has also opened a second facility in North Carolina.

- ASG Software Solutions has its worldwide headquarters here in Naples. Just as its name implies, it provides large businesses with software solutions.

Other major employers in our area include Publix, a grocery store with many locations throughout town, Walmart, which has several super centers in greater Fort Myers, and First Florida Integrity Bank, which is headquartered in Southwest Florida.

Top 25 Employers in Southwest Florida

Rank	Company Name	2017 Employment
1	Lee County School District	13,723
2	Lee Health	13,595
3	Lee County Local Government	9,044
4	Publix Super Market	7,183
5	NCH Healthcare System	7,017
6	Collier County School District	6,422
7	Walmart Supercenter	5,271
8	Collier County Local Government	5,011
9	Florida Gulf Coast University	4,211
10	Bayfront Health	3,060
11	Charlotte County School District	2,655
12	Arthrex, Inc.	2,500
13	McDonald's	2,423
14	Charlotte County Local Government	2,394
15	City of Cape Coral	2,213
16	Winn-Dixie	2,149
17	US Sugar	2,100
18	Palm Automotive	2,050
19	Home Depot	2,040

20	City of Naples	1,867
21	Florida SouthWestern State College	1,441
22	Gartner, Inc.	1,200
23	Walgreens	1,171
24	Target	1,150
25	Chico's Fas Inc.	1,147

Source: Florida Department of Economic Opportunity

Lots of Business Resources to Benefit Your Company and Yourself

Entrepreneurs in our community will find a ton of support .

Lee County Economic Development

Fort Myers Economic Development

The Greater Fort Myers Chamber of Commerce offers classes, resources, contacts, and videos to help you start or grow a business, while

Southwest Florida Economic Development Alliance

Florida Small Business Development Center at FGCU

Small Business Resource Network – Southwest Florida

SCORE Southwest Florida, the non-profit organization pairs you with an entrepreneurial mentor of similar background to guide you through all-things business.

Local business publications give insight into the area's trends, spotlight local up-and-coming companies, and offer tips for success. They include:

Gulfshore Business
Southwest Florida Business Today
Business Observer
Business Currents

Hertz Global Headquarters at Home in Estero

A primary factor in the decision to relocate from New Jersey to SW Florida was the welcoming economic climate of Florida, and Estero in particular, according to John Boyd, a corporate relocation consultant based in Princeton, N.J.

"This out-migration out of New Jersey is real," he said. "Mercedes left a year after Hertz. The outflow of huge corporations from the state isn't over. People are leaving in droves."

For example, he said, Mercedes-Benz, the German car manufacturer, is in the process of moving its U.S. headquarters from Montvale, N.J., to Sandy Springs, Ga.

"We term operating costs in New Jersey as confiscatory," Boyd said. "It's an extremely expensive place to do business."

As for Estero, Boyd said, it benefits from Florida's aggressive incentive program to bring in corporate headquarters.

Added to that, he said, the Estero area has the lowest business operating costs of any suburban office market in the East.

Part of the reason we attract businesses here is our economic development offices work together to attract businesses here and then work together to make the relocation process seamless.

Corporations and small business owners see the benefits of:

- Talented workforce and educational pipeline to educate employees in emerging fields like technology, pharmaceuticals, "Educational Assets"

- Easily accessible international airport

- Low cost of living for employees and executives

- Infrastructure that supports your business today and in the future expansion

Small Business Support

Our colleges and universities work hand and hand with new business through Small Business Development programs that help new businesses thrive. In addition, the Service Corps of Retired Executives (SCORE) www.score.org is extremely valuable for local startups.

Horizon Council

This foundation is all about optimizing the local business environment for the benefit of existing and future businesses.

As they explain it:

> The Horizon Council is a public-private board established in 1991 to advise the Lee County Board of Commissioners on economic development issues. The Council has up to 80 members representing cities; chambers of commerce; economic development and trade organizations; community, business, and education organizations; along with various officers and at-large members.

> The Horizon Council is the voice of business in Lee County. The Council's mission is to improve Lee County's business environment, retain and encourage expansion of existing

businesses, and attract new and diversified employers. It is the only public-private partnership of Lee County Government and business leaders.

Find them online:
www.leecountybusiness.com/about-us/horizon-council

Employment Market and Top Employers

If you are relocating to Lee County and need to seek employment, CareerSource of Southwest Florida is a great resource to help you find the right career in the Southwest Florida job market which covers 5 counties: Charlotte, Collier, Glades, Hendry, and Lee.

Another great job-finding resource is Employ Florida.

The best way to find your dream career in the sunshine state is through networking. This might be difficult to do before physically moving here, but with today's technology it can be done. First let's take a look of the Hot Jobs List for Lee County.

Occupation / Position	Percent Annual Growth	Annual Openings	Average Wage
Architectural and engineering managers	1.95	151	$55.91
Business teachers, postsecondary	2.21	109	$44.61
Computer and information systems managers	1.6	174	$62.22
Dietitians and nutritionists	1.91	66	$26.26
Financial analysts	1.6	157	$33.34
Human resources managers	1.84	72	$49.79
Logistician	3.38	182	$32.11
Machinists	1.58	64	$19.92
Marketing managers	2.1	135	$52.62
Motorboat mechanics	2.08	53	$22.50
Nursing assistants	3.39	60	$14.94
Pharmacy technicians	2.78	65	$15.36
Software developers, system software	1.73	1.93	$44.30
Special education teachers, kindergarten and elementary	1.66	127	$29.07
Special education teachers, middle school	1.66	52	$28.67

High demand jobs lists like the one above can be found online at CareerSource of Southwest Florida. They create annual reports that not only tell you the jobs that are in demand, but what education and training you need to have to get these jobs. Find this information and more at www.careersourcesouthwestflorida.com/occupations-in-demand. The reports include schooling information along with program specifics like grant eligibility, student costs, program length, credit hours, and degree certificate needed. Lee County is focused on developing talent!

Schooling, specified certification, and previous on the job experience is the foundation you need to find the best employment offers.

Self-directed job search and virtual recruiter

Once you have the skills, certification, degree or training required for a job in southwest Florida it is time to learn the secret of successful job hunting. The secret is that 75% to 80% of jobs are unadvertised! So how do you find these jobs? Well, you need to know where to look.

Jobs become available because businesses are starting up or expanding. Job opportunities also appear thanks to recent vacancies in existing companies when an employee has quit, been fired, gotten promoted, retired or relocated. Contact a local group for your profession and start networking.

Because hiring is such a big expense, typically organizations will search within their professional networks. Be in the know by getting involved in some of these networking and professional groups.

Pretty much every occupation has a professional association with an online presence. The key is to connect and become active with the local chapter for your profession. Then you can be among the first to learn of great new opportunities.

An excellent place to connect is the CareerSource of Southwest Florida via its Professional Career Network (PCN),

- The Professional Career Network (PCN)at CareerSource of Southwest Florida offers networking, job referrals, resume critiques, career counseling, coaching, workshops, and exposure to local employers.

Business Resources for Local Companies

Economic Development in Southwest Florida has never been stronger. The Gulf Coast counties work together to draw business to our coast versus competing over them.

Let our economic development offices help your business flourish in the sunshine state.

Here is a list of valuable resources:

- Lee County Economic Development Office
  www.leecountybusiness.com

- Cape Coral Economic Development Office
  www.capecoral.net/edo

- Small Business Resource Network
  www.sbrn.org

CHAPTER 10
GETTING SETTLED

Getting Connected

The internet makes things so much easier and moving to a new city is no exception. You can find many great tips about SWFL from this book, online resources, and through friends or relatives that you have living in this area.

Not every detail can be covered in a book and the Greater Fort Myers area is constantly growing, evolving, and becoming even greater. So, I extend to my readers an invitation to get connected to me through our website www.MovingtoFortMyersGuide.com.

Let's help you get connected!

The best way to get rooted and connected to your new community is through the things you value and love the most. You can get connected through your profession, your pets, and/or your kids. You name it there is a sunny and welcoming spot for you to get to know dozens of new colleagues and friends.

The Greater Fort Myers Area has several professional/civic networks that will facilitate your connecting personally and professionally:

- Greater Fort Myers Chamber of Commerce (www.fortmyers.org)

- Cape Coral Chamber of Commerce
  (www.capecoralchamber.com)

- Bonita Springs Chamber of Commerce
  (www.bonitaspringschamber.com)

- Estero Chamber of Commerce (https://esterochamber.org)

- Young Professionals of SWFL (www.ypswfl.com)

- 13 separate BNI Networks (www.bniswfl.com)

- 10 Rotary Clubs (www.capecoralrotary.com &
  www.rotaryfortmyers.org)

- Association for Talent Development (www.atdswfl.org)

- Christian Chamber of Commerce (www.hischamber.org)

- Hispanic Chamber or Commerce
  (www.hispanicchamberflorida.org)

Our area has a superb philanthropic organization, the Southwest Florida Community Foundation (www.floridacommunity.com), which has invested $5.4 million into our community through grants and programs in 2017 alone! They assist in funding things we all care about: animals, educations, people, economic development, environment, and the arts.

On a purely social level you can seek out a variety of groups of varying interest on meetup.com or Facebook.com groups. I prefer to just go about my daily tasks and be friendly and chat with people. You never know who you might meet!

Making the Move

Establish Residency

One of the first things you can do to establish residency is to go to the Clerk of Courts and obtain a Declaration of Domicile. It will legally establish your new home as your residency which will then allow you to file for your homestead exemption, enroll children in public school, private school or in college. www.leeclerk.org

Obtaining Your Florida Driver's License

To obtain your Florida driver's license you must have the proper documentation regulated federally by the Department of Homeland Security's Real ID Act to prove citizenship/immigration status. Visit www.leetc.com/driver-licenses/document-requirements for specific requirements. Fees, branch locations, and hours can be found here www.flhsmv.gov/locations/lee.

Registering Your Vehicle

Next you will need to obtain your automobile insurance from a licensed Florida insurance agency. Take the proof of your insurance along with your vehicle title to get your new Florida license plates and complete the vehicle registration process. For fee schedule, locations, and wait times visit www.leetc.com/vehicles-vessels/title-and-registration-fees. Early mornings are usually your best bet!

Registering to Vote

Once you have your Florida driver's license, you can register to vote. Visit the www.registertovoteflorida.gov website and have your Florida driver's license and the last 4 digits of your social security number ready to complete the process online.

Registering Your Pets

Don't forget to register your pets! Dogs, cats, and ferrets require a rabies certificate in order to get registered. You can bring your proof of rabies vaccination to the County Domestic Animal Services, 5600 Banner Drive, Fort Myers, FL 33912 to obtain your registration and rabies tag. You can also have this done through a Lee County Veterinarian that issues licenses. It is also a great idea to have your animal micro-chipped since moving and a new environment could be stressful for new animals. Contact www.leegov.com/animalservices/licensing for more information.

CHAPTER 11

WEB LINKS AND EXTRAS

Key Resources: Websites & Phone Numbers

Visit our website for links to a wealth of Fort Myers & surrounding area resources.
www.facebook.com/movingtofortmyers

IMPORTANT CONTACT INFORMATION AND WEBSITE LINKS:

Local Media

- NBC-2 www.nbc-2.com

- Wink TV www.winknews.com

- ABC-7 www.abc-7.com

- Fox 4 Now www.fox4now.com

- WGCU/PBS www.wgcu.org

- Government Access
  www.leegov.com/technologyservices/leetv/watchleetv

Print Media

- *News-Press* www.news-press.com

- *Florida Weekly* www.floridaweekly.com

Business Assistance

Greater Fort Myers Chamber of Commerce
www.fortmyers.org
239-332-3624

Cape Coral Chamber of Commerce
www.capecoralchamber.com
239-549-6900

Lehigh Acres Chamber of Commerce
www.lehighacreschamber.org
239-369-3322

North Fort Myers Chamber of Commerce
www.nfmchamber.com
239-997-9111

Sanibel & Captiva Island Chamber of Commerce
www.sanibel-captiva.org
239-472-1080

Fort Myers Beach Chamber of Commerce
www.fortmyersbeach.org
239-454-7500

Estero Chamber of Commerce
www.esterochamber.org
239-948-7990

Bonita Springs Chamber of Commerce
www.bonitaspringschamber.com
239-992-2943

Lee County Economic Development
www.leecountybusiness.com
239-338-3161

Police Departments

Lee County Sheriff Department
14750 Six Mile Cypress Pkwy.
Fort Myers, FL 33912
(239) 477-1000 / www.sheriffleefl.org

Cape Coral Police Department
1100 Cultural Park Blvd
Cape Coral, FL 33990
(239) 574-3223 / www.capecoral.net

Fort Myers Police Department
2210 Widman Way
Fort Myers, FL 33901
(239) 321-7700 /www.fmpolice.com

Sanibel Police Department
800 Dunlop Road
Sanibel, Florida 33957
(239) 472-3111 / www.mysanibel.com

Hospitals

Lee Memorial Hospital
2776 Cleveland Avenue, Fort Myers, FL 33901
(239) 343-2000 / www.leehealth.org

HealthPark Medical Center
9981 S. HealthPark Drive, Fort Myers, FL 33908
(239) 343-5000 / www.leehealth.org

Cape Coral Hospital
636 Del Prado Boulevard, Cape Coral, FL 33990
(239) 424-2000 / www.leehealth.org

Gulf Coast Medical Center
13681 Doctors Way, Fort Myers FL, 33912
(239) 677-4251 / www.leehealth.org

Lehigh Regional Medical Center
1500 Lee Boulevard, Lehigh Acres, FL 33936
(239) 369-2101 / www.lehighregional.com

Lee County VA Healthcare Center
2489 Diplomat Parkway East
Cape Coral, FL 33909
Phone: 239-652-1800 / www.baypines.va.gov
Veterans crisis hotline (800) 273-8255 (Press 1).

ACKNOWLEDGMENTS

I would not have been able to write this book without the invaluable assistance of local experts who have shared their knowledge to benefit our readers who want to know everything there is to know about making Greater Fort Myers their home.

In particular, we are so grateful for the assistance of the following organizations and individuals:

Bob McFarlane, CEO of The McFarlane Barney Group, and his team provided invaluable insights into downtown Fort Myers living, particularly understanding the richness of high-rise home choices by the water-from the very affordable to the very expensive. In addition, his team at the Prima Luce Group provided remarkably beautiful images including our cover shot that shows the diversity of our downtown choices. Bob also wrote an inspiring sidebar about downtown, high-rise living.

Kellie Burns, NBC-2 news anchor, wrote a wonderful foreword that explains her 25-year love affair with the Fort Myers area. Although she had not intended to spend a lifetime here, she loves Southwest Florida so much that she's made it her forever home.

Sarah E. Craine, the author of *Bucket List for Foodies* for Southwest Florida, delivered a delightful sidebar about all the wonderful "fest" events we have every year. Thanks to Sarah, we learn all about great food, great spirits, and great fun in Greater Fort Myers.

Ruth Condit, owner of Ruth Condit Interiors, provided unique insights into selecting just the right combination of design elements to create a wonderful look for your new home's interior.

Lydia Black, Executive Director of the Alliance for the Arts, shared her wisdom about the incredible selection of professional and amateur arts activities.

Brian Culbertson, head of the Culbertson Agency, provided invaluable information about insurance requirements that are specific to Southwest Florida, including the potential need for flood insurance.

Dr. Suzanne Felt, a certified Emergency Medicine Physician at Lee Health, offered a marvelous blueprint for working your way through the complexities of our regional healthcare system.

Kathy Cole, a married mother of two, provided insights into Lee County's school choice program and how each of her very different children benefited from unique choices.

Chris Black, owner of Winged Foot Title, explained for potential buyers what professionals you may need to select in order to successfully complete the purchase of local home.

Finally, many thanks to my publisher, Voyager Media, Inc., for helping me work through the complexities of writing a book that will provide real and lasting value to its readers.

LAURA PIERCE HESS BIOGRAPHY

Our author, Laura Hess, was fortunate enough to grow up in Southwest Florida and was raised in Cape Coral, where she attended middle school and high school. She attended Edison State College in Fort Myers.

She loves this part of the world, particularly greater Fort Myers. So, this book has been a labor of love for Laura.

Laura spent many years working with prospective homeowners in Southwest Florida to get them the mortgages they need to purchase the homes that they really wanted. So, she understands the essential information that they need to settle quickly into our area.

She also served as the Web Marketing Manager for the Internet Services Group of Florida, LLC helping them grow their web marketing division. She created lots of content in the form of e-books, news releases, blog posts, and social media updates.

Laura brings her extensive knowledge of living in Southwest Florida to the pages of *Moving to Greater Fort Myers: The Un-Tourist Guide®* in order to enable new and future residents to settle quickly and easily into their new communities.

She is happily married to Jeffrey Hess and the mother of two wonderful children.

Made in the USA
Middletown, DE
30 November 2021

53872342R00080